GW00775600

The JOY of being Anglican

"Having visited virtually every part of the worldwide Anglican Communion, I have seen the many faces of Anglicanism. This book captures something of the distinctive spirit of a joyful global family. Not angels but Anglicans, whatever their nationality."

Terry Waite CBE

Fifteen writers reflect on Anglicanism, what it means
to them personally, and on the joy of being Anglican

The JOY of being Anglican

anglican

Published by Redemptorist Publications
Alphonsus House, Chawton, Hampshire, GU34 3HQ, UK
Tel. +44 (0)1420 88222, Fax. +44 (0)1420 88805
Email: rp@rpbooks.co.uk, www.rpbooks.co.uk

A registered charity limited by guarantee
Registered in England 3261721

Copyright © Redemptorist Publications 2017
First published October 2017

Edited by Caroline Hodgson and Heather Smith
Designed by Eliana Thompson

ISBN 978-0-85231-477-7

All rights reserved. No part of this publication may be reproduced, stored in a retrieval system,
or transmitted in any form or by any means, electronic, mechanical, photocopying, recording or
otherwise, without prior permission in writing from Redemptorist Publications.

The moral right of the contributors to be identified as the authors of this work has been asserted in
accordance with the Copyright, Designs and Patents Act 1988.

Every effort has been made to trace copyright holders and to obtain their permission for the use of
copyright material. The publisher apologises for any errors or omissions and would be grateful for
notification of any corrections that should be incorporated in future reprints or editions of this book.

A CIP catalogue record for this book is available from the British Library.

The publisher gratefully acknowledges permission to use the following copyright material:

Excerpts from the New Revised Standard Version of the Bible: Anglicised Edition, © 1989, 1995,
Division of Christian Education of the National Council of the Churches of Christ in the United
States of America. Used by permission. All rights reserved.

Common Worship material, as taken from the Church of England website,
is © The Archbishops' Council, 2000, and is reproduced by permission.
All rights reserved. Copyright@churchofengland.org

Photography:
Photo of Jeni Parsons on page 16 by Rob Lawrence-Jones
Photo of Gillian Cooper on page 23 by Alessandro Repetti
Photo of Paul Kerensa on page 38 by Steve Fanstone
Photo of John Witcombe on page 73 courtesy of Coventry Cathedral
Photo of Daniel Newman on page 85 by Gerry Lynch
Photo of Victor and Nolavy Osoro on page 95 by Veronique Razafitiana
Photo of Muthuraj Swamy on page 112 by Graham Kings

Printed by GPS Colour Graphics Ltd, Belfast.

The editors gratefully
acknowledge the help,
guidance and support
of the following people:

Gillian Cooper

Prudence Dailey,
Chairman of the
Prayer Book Society

The Revd Anders Litzell,
Prior of the Community
of St Anselm

The Revd Dr Patsy McGregor

Max Serjeant

A note from the editors

by Caroline Hodgson and Heather Smith

The original idea for *The Joy of Being Anglican* was conceived by Fr Denis McBride, himself an author, scripture scholar and Redemptorist Publications' Director of Publishing. As he handed the baton to us, as we later agreed, we both had a clear idea of the kind of book he had in mind – namely a multi-author work celebrating Anglicanism from different perspectives. It all seemed straightforward. Little did we know, however, what a rollercoaster of a journey it would take us on – often unnerving, occasionally a white-knuckle ride, ultimately exhilarating. Along the way – the ups and downs, twists and turns – we learned a huge amount, not only about Anglicanism, but also about the huge range of approaches that Anglicans have towards their Communion and their faith – and towards writing about the subject.

We began by scratching our heads as to who might contribute to such a project. We decided that it would be good to ask each contributor to focus on a particular aspect of Anglicanism, to bring focus, depth and variety. Working within that framework, we agreed not to make the brief too directive or restrictive, to give each contributor freedom to interpret it for themselves. Moreover, each was presented with a number of chapter titles and asked to choose the one which most inspired him or her. It struck us later that this was a very Anglican way of going about things!

Just when we had what we considered a good mix of chapters, we were pulled up for privileging Church of England voices over Anglicanism in other parts of the Communion. We were reminded that the Archbishop of Canterbury points out that the average Anglican is a black sub-Saharan woman in her thirties. It was a humbling realisation that we had not given her a voice. Happily, Graham Kings, the Mission Theologian for the Anglican Communion, who has contributed the foreword to this book, was on hand to introduce us to Anglicans in Africa (Lydia Mwakini, who has written on "The Joy of Education for an Anglican Woman") and India (Muthuraj Swamy, who has written on "The Joy of Relationships for an Anglican"). We feel their contributions have immensely enriched the book.

Having broadened the book's scope, however, we then became concerned that it would turn out to be a mixed bag of chapters that varied greatly in tone and style – and indeed that is the case. However, we believe that far from being a weakness, this is one of its strengths. Victor and Nolavy Osoro, for example, who have written about "The Joy of Service", live and work in the Diocese of Toliara, in the south of Madagascar. As you can read, their day-to-day lives and ministry are about as far removed as possible from the experience of the majority of those who will read *The Joy of Being Anglican*. Most Anglicans do not have to walk barefoot through rice fields, as Victor does, and don't tend to interpret dreams as messages from God, as Nolavy relates. Perhaps it wouldn't be such a bad idea…

But you don't have to travel far to learn about the diversity of the Anglican Communion and its people. Not many of us have done lambing "out in the field under the stars or in the pouring rain", as Jeni Parsons recounts in her chapter on "The Joy of the Seasons", or spent their childhood and teenage years in crumbling vicarages, doing O level revision by candlelight during the strikes of the 1970s, as Ruth Gledhill relates in "The Joy of the Family".

Some of the chapters are obviously about "Church", and invite us to look anew at aspects of Anglicanism that we might take for granted. In "The Joy of English Church Buildings" Gillian Cooper shares her passion for church architecture, contending that, "The buildings themselves preach the Gospel in ways we do not always realise or understand." What a wonderful idea, that the fabric of the building which for PCCs often comes to represent a budgetary headache and a never-ending schedule of repairs and maintenance, could itself bring us the message of the Gospel.

Other chapters may surprise you by coming at the subject from a quirky angle. Humour, for example, might not strike you as a very Anglican subject, but Paul Kerensa begs to differ, and his chapter, "The Joy of Laughter", written in the form of a diary, makes a strong case for seeing the funny side.

What was unusual at Ronnie Barker's funeral? You might not expect this book to answer that question, but you can find out in Leigh Nixon's chapter. Written in the form of an interview, Leigh brings us a privileged behind-the-scenes glimpse into the life of a chorister at Westminster Abbey, where he has sung at many high-profile royal and state occasions.

Gillian, Heather, Jeni, Leigh, Lydia, Nolavy, Paul, Ruth and Victor have brought their own stories and experiences to the book. Other contributors have taken a more scholarly approach, each with infectious enthusiasm for their chosen subject. Rachel Mann, for example, shows us that there is joy and beauty in the "porous boundaries and wideness" of Anglican poetry, and invites us to revisit the poetry of Donne, Herbert, Rossetti, Auden, R. S. Thomas, Rowan Williams and others.

Meanwhile, Muthuraj Swamy makes the case that the essence of Anglican identity is that it is relational. His vision of Anglicanism is of a web of relationships, holding "millions of Christians… from many diverse national, ethnic, linguistic, cultural, social, political and economic backgrounds… united in a relationship that goes back for generations and hundreds of years".

Simon Cowling's deep love of Anglican liturgy is evident in his chapter and goes right back to his childhood. He challenges the view that "worship is the province of those who have dispensed with liturgy", or that liturgy places "burdensome restrictions on the activity of the Holy Spirit".

For Daniel Newman, the liturgy that has inspired him since childhood is the very Anglican Book of Common Prayer. In his chapter, Daniel goes through Morning and Evening Prayer, looking at how each part of the Order of Service relates to our lives. As he contends: "Anyone who thinks that the Prayer Book encourages an unhealthily low view of ourselves (so-called worm theology) has not spent enough time meditating on the Comfortable Words."

A book on any church would hardly be complete without looking at scripture. Trevor Dennis encourages to look afresh at familiar stories, such as the Garden of Eden, which he and his students excavated from "beneath the rubble" of doctrine, to unearth a "sparkling, poignant tale".

John Witcombe brings us the subject of vocation, without which the Anglican Communion would not exist. He looks at how both clergy and laity can bring their own special gifts to the service of that great institution that has served its people down the years, and which, we pray, will continue to do.

Samuel Johnson famously said that "When a man is tired of London, he is tired of life." Could a similar claim not be made for the Anglican Communion? We cannot claim to have covered every subject – many remain on our list of chapters which have not, so far, been written. On our journey of discovery, our rollercoaster, we learned that there is much, much more joy in Anglicanism than could be written in one book by fifteen writers. We hope that we have given you a tantalising glimpse of what you will find in the pages of this book, and that these insights might lead you to reflect on what Anglicanism means to you personally, and possibly to discover, or rediscover, that there is real joy in being Anglican.

Fifteen writers reflect on Anglicanism, what it means to them personally, and on the joy of being Anglican

Contents

Foreword by the Rt Revd Dr Graham Kings,
Mission Theologian in the Anglican Communion 12

1   The Joy of the Seasons for an Anglican
    by Jeni Parsons 16

2   The Joy of English Church Buildings for an Anglican
    by Gillian Cooper 23

3   The Joy of the Liturgy for an Anglican
    by Simon Cowling 30

4   The Joy of Laughter for an Anglican
    by Paul Kerensa 38

5   The Joy of Poetry for an Anglican
    by Rachel Mann 47

6   The Joy of the Family for an Anglican
    by Ruth Gledhill 56

7   The Joy of Scripture for an Anglican
    by Trevor Dennis 65

8   The Joy of Vocation for an Anglican
    by John Witcombe 73

9   The Joy of the Prayer Book for an Anglican
    by Daniel Newman 85

10 The Joy of Service for an Anglican
    by Victor and Nolavy Osoro 95

11 The Joy of Prayer for an Anglican
    by Heather Smith 104

12 The Joy of Relationships for an Anglican
    by Muthuraj Swamy 112

13 The Joy of Education for an Anglican Woman
    by Lydia Mwaniki 123

14 The Joy of Church Music for an Anglican
    by Leigh Nixon 132

Foreword

by the Rt Revd Dr Graham Kings

Mission Theologian in the Anglican Communion
and Honorary Fellow of Durham University

I commend this imaginative book with joy. The diverse chapters from England and around the Anglican Communion, on various themes, are a delight to read. Buildings, service, scripture, liturgy, family, poetry, laughter, music, vocation, seasons, prayer and relationships all come alive through multiple voices. The editors and authors are to be congratulated on bringing to fruition an endeavour full of vitality.

Thomas Traherne (1637-1674), an Anglican priest, theologian and poet who served a parish near Hereford in the middle of the seventeenth century, wrote a spiritually profound book, *Centuries of Meditations*. This was first published only in 1908, its manuscript having been left undiscovered for centuries and found in a barrow of books about to be trashed.[1] He wrote of the beauty of nature and of the soul's capacity for joy:

> You never enjoy the world aright, till the Sea itself floweth in your veins, till you are clothed with the heavens, and crowned with the stars: and perceive yourself to be the sole heir of the whole world, and more than so, because men are in it who are every one sole heirs as well as you. Till you can sing and rejoice and delight in God, as misers do in gold, and Kings in sceptres, you never enjoy the world.[2]

For Traherne, the joy of worship led into the joy of mission:

> Yet, further, you never enjoy the world aright, till you so love the beauty of enjoying it, that you are covetous and earnest to persuade others to enjoy it.[3]

---

1 Denise Inge, in *Happiness and Holiness: Thomas Traherne and His Writings* (Norwich: Canterbury Press, 2008) tells the story of this discovery, and also of further manuscripts of Traherne which Jeremy Maule and, later, she, found in Lambeth Palace Library.

2 Thomas Traherne, *Centuries of Meditations* (London: Faith Press, 1960), 14.

3 Traherne, 1960, 15.

On 19 August 1945, C. S. Lewis (1898-1963), an Anglican layman, English don at Oxford and great admirer of Traherne,[4] wrote to Mrs Ellis:

> Real joy… jumps under one's ribs and tickles down one's back and makes one forget meals and keeps one (delightedly) sleepless o'nights.[5]

This handwritten letter was discovered inside a secondhand copy of Lewis's book, *The Problem of Pain*. A few years later, Lewis wrote his memoir, *Surprised by Joy*, and included this passage:

> Joy must be sharply distinguished both from Happiness and Pleasure. Joy (in my sense) has indeed one characteristic, and one only, in common with them; the fact that anyone who has experienced it will want it again.[6]

Perhaps one way of looking at this concept is that peace is joy resting and joy is peace dancing. The Anglican daily liturgy, drawing on Benedictine roots, is permeated with joy. Morning Prayer begins with the call to worship, Psalm 95, the Venite, after its opening Latin word:

> O come, let us sing to the Lord;
> let us heartily rejoice in the rock of our salvation.

The third canticle of Morning Prayer is Psalm 100, the Jubilate:

> O be joyful in the Lord, all the earth;
> serve the Lord with gladness;
>   and come before his presence with a song.

The central canticle of Evening Prayer is Mary's Magnificat (Luke 1:46-55):

> My soul proclaims the greatness of the Lord,
> my spirit rejoices in God my Saviour.

Of the Gospel writers, Luke in particular picks out the theme of joy. The birth stories are shot through with it. The angel tells Zechariah, "You will have joy and gladness, and many will rejoice at his birth" (Luke 1:14); his wife, Elizabeth, tells Mary, "As soon as I heard the sound of your greeting, the child in my womb leaped for joy" (1:44), and her friends rejoice with her at the

---

4 On 23 December 1941, C. S. Lewis wrote to his friend, Arthur Greeves: "I'm re-reading Traherne's Centuries *of Meditations* which I think almost the most beautiful book (in prose, I mean, excluding poets) in English." Quoted in Walter Hooper (ed.), *They Stand Together: The Letters of C.S.Lewis to Arthur Greeves (1914-1963)* (London: William Collins, 1979), 492.
5 C. S. Lewis, letter to Mrs Ellis, "Unseen C. S. Lewis Letter Defines his Notion of Joy", The Guardian (9 December 2014).
6 C. S. Lewis, *Surprised by Joy. The Shape of My Early Life* (London: Geoffrey Bles, 1955), 24.

birth of John (1:58); Mary's response to God, the Magnificat, is full of joy; the angels greet the shepherds with "good news of great joy for all the people" (2:10); in Luke's version of the beatitudes, Jesus says, "Rejoice in that day and leap for joy, for surely your reward is great in heaven" (6:23); Jesus "rejoiced in the Holy Spirit" (10:21); the parable of the lost sheep, lost coin and lost son all mention joy at being found (15:5. 9-10. 32); during his entry to Jerusalem, the disciples "began to praise God joyfully with a loud voice" (19:37); at his resurrection, "in their joy they were disbelieving and still wondering," (24:41); and after his ascension, returned to Jerusalem "with great joy" (24:52). Thus Luke begins and ends his Gospel with this theme.

Of Paul's epistles, his letter to the Philippians in particular resounds with encouragements to rejoice. This is ironic, as he is imprisoned in Rome. Yet he is, "constantly praying with joy in every one of my prayers" (1:4). He continues on the theme of joy by declaring that "Christ is proclaimed in every way, whether out of false motives or true; and in that I rejoice… and I will continue to rejoice" (1:18); "make my joy complete: be of the same mind…" (2:2). Even if he were to die he says, "I am glad and rejoice with all of you – and in the same way you also must be glad and rejoice with me" (2:17-18). He is sending Epaphroditus "in order that you may rejoice at seeing him again, and… Welcome him then in the Lord with joy" (2:28-29). He ends that section by urging the Philippians, "Finally, my brothers and sisters, rejoice in the Lord" (3:1), calling them "my joy and crown" (4:1) and repeating his encouragement to "Rejoice in the Lord, always; again I will say, Rejoice" (4:4). Finally, now that they have revived their concern for him, he says, "I rejoice in the Lord greatly" (4:10).

The traditional phrase used to describe the Anglican tradition is "Catholic and Reformed". Too often the middle word "and" passes unnoticed. Connecting words are crucial, humble and worth contemplating. They introduce links between polarities by contributing "three-ness to duality". If we try to replace "and" with the word "or", we would soon see its significance.

Perhaps Anglicans in England have four founding patron saints of this little word "and":

- *Thomas Cranmer* (1489-1556), in the Book of Common Prayer, reshaped patristic prayers in the light of renewed evangelical theology.

- *Richard Hooker* (1554-1600), in his *Lawes of Ecclesiastical Politie*, countered both Roman and Puritan demands with God's layered wisdom.

- *Lancelot Andrewes* (1555-1626), brought erudition and insight to the King James Version of the Bible and sermons before the Royal Court.

- *George Herbert* (1593-1633), in his temperate prose and allusive poetry, expressed profound spirituality in subtle rhetoric.

Anglicanism, thanks be to God, is now global. As well as drawing on British authors, this book introduces us to theologians and ministers around the world who are developing their own insights. There may be tensions in the Communion, but also profound relationships of trust and mutuality.

Celebrating and discussing theological insights on mission with Anglicans around the world has renewed my joy in Christ and appreciation of worldwide Anglicanism.

As we approach the 2020 Lambeth Conference, when Anglican bishops from six continents will gather at Canterbury, I pray that this book may enliven minds and envision imaginations to rejoice in the traditions which interweave being Catholic and Reformed.

Having begun with Traherne, I conclude with the final verse of George Herbert's poem, "The Call":

> Come, my Joy, my Love, my Heart:
> Such a Joy, as none can move:
> Such a Love, as none can part:
> Such a Heart, as joys in love.[7]

Graham Kings is a bishop and theologian. He studied at the universities of Oxford, Cambridge and Utrecht, and served as curate in Harlesden, London, Vice Principal of St Andrew's College, Kabare, Kenya, founding Director of the Cambridge Centre for Christianity Worldwide, Vicar of Islington and Bishop of Sherborne. Currently, he lives in London and is Mission Theologian in the Anglican Communion, working at Lambeth Palace Library, and has an Honorary Fellowship at Durham University. He has written poetry and books on the theology of mission, Kenyan liturgy and art and theology. He is married to Alison, a psychotherapist, and they have three daughters.

---

7 George Herbert, "The Call", in Helen Wilcox (ed.), The English Poems of George Herbert (Cambridge: University Press, 2007), 538.

The Joy of the Seasons for an Anglican

by the Revd Canon Dr Jeni Parsons

Jeni is a retired parish priest. She has worked on a number of outer housing estates in the West Midlands, Worcester and Gloucester. Before that, as a layperson she worked in the Diocese of Lincoln as an adult education officer and then trained ordinands with the Aston Training Scheme. Now as a farmer in west Wales, on a very old tiny farm, she ministers locally when needed and writes when there's time. She is a left-handed Australian, a coracler and supports Wales in the rugby.

It was the colour of the Anglican Communion that drew me as a child newly arrived from Australia in 1960. At a Church of England primary school I was drawn into mystery and a new language through learning hymns and then the liturgical colours. I learned that the colours, purple, red, white, gold, and green, changed throughout the year according to the season, mostly in blocks of several Sundays, but disrupted by a spattering of white and red from time to time, as saints and martyrs had their days. The new knowledge gave me the edge over my parents whenever we visited a church, and I liked that power very much at the age of seven. That was a mean kind of joy, but delicious!

I was an atheist teenager as a local church chorister and loved the colours still, but was introduced to the smells of the seasons in the village churches round about. Of course harvest, with its rich smell of apples on the church windowsills, was the strongest, but exploration in the local town with the school choir brought the experience of incense on some of those special gold days, when we would sing a Mozart Mass setting and the best vestments were worn. And in that High-Church Anglican place new colours appeared – rose, Sarum blue, black. Long before I began to find my way to a faith of my own, baptism and confirmation, the seasons were profound in my life and now I'm old they remain as a focus when the churchy words sometimes bore me.

The liturgical year in the Anglican Communion focuses on the life and ministry of Christ, the beginning of the Church and those who first spread it beyond Jerusalem. It is a way of recalling what is in this great story, with the changing liturgical colours being an *aide memoire* for the people. Many of the symbols from the Christian past have been reintroduced in the last fifty years, to enable participation in the activity of that story. An Advent wreath in Advent, when candles are lit as the weeks progress to remind people of the patriarchs and matriarchs of the faith, the prophets of the Bible, John the Baptist and the Virgin Mary, culminating on Christmas Eve or Christmas Day with the lighting of the central white candle for Christ, has been a teaching mechanism and a thing of beauty in itself.

The crib scene, used in many churches but dating back to Francis of Assisi perhaps, draws people into the vision of that birth. In Epiphany there is sometimes a set of figures of the Wise Men, who have been making their way through the church to arrive at the crib on 6 January. At Candlemas there is a blessing of candles, often a procession and sometimes a renewal of baptismal vows. Ash Wednesday sees the burning of last year's palm crosses to make ash for the service of imposition, when we are marked and reminded of our death, and then come the long days of Lent, when many people give up certain pleasures to focus more simply on the life of Jesus. Holy Week sees a procession perhaps, palm crosses blessed, a meal on Maundy Thursday and a watch late into the night as the story of Jesus' arrest is lived out again. Then comes the reading of the Good Friday story and a time of meditation, the waiting of Easter Eve with its new fire and the new paschal candle of Easter Day. The work of the Holy Spirit is time for celebration at Pentecost, and then on Trinity Sunday we see a return to the green vestments and a rest from the fizzy excitement of the story, until we reach Advent again. Some Anglican churches will not do very much of this activity but others rejoice in this way of telling and living the story.

As a retired Anglican priest now living in rural west Wales, I am also a full member of my local independent Welsh-speaking chapel. Here, seasons are barely observed, and I find that fascinating also. The agricultural seasons are deep in all our lives locally, since most of us farm or grow vegetables, but the seasons of the Christian Church, beyond Christmas and Easter, are not observed in the services. Instead there is a deeper devotion to the specialness of Sunday, when older farmers are slightly embarrassed to admit to shearing or haymaking on that day. The lingering awareness that not all days are the same is powerful even in those whose chapel-going has long since ceased except for Thanksgiving (celebrated with no fruit, vegetables or other produce in evidence). Being thankful for harvest in this context makes sense of lives lived by the agricultural seasons and an awareness of God being deep in there somewhere. I still take Anglican services locally when required, where the liturgical seasons are observed, and it allows me the space to be in this local chapel in a new way, because it's the natural seasons that bring me to God rather than the scraps of coloured cloth which announce the seasons in the church.

I'm a smallholder and the agricultural year, linked in the northern hemisphere with the Christian calendar, is profoundly important to me now in a way that it wasn't before. I saw something on Twitter recently, tweeted from a rural conference, describing it as a "whistle-stop tour" of the agricultural year – wassail, Imbolc, midsummer, Lammas. I was interested to see a mix of pagan, Christian and agricultural seasons in the one sentence, and yet the connections are obvious: Imbolc and Candlemas happen at the same time and both speak of light; Lammas is a harvest celebration for Christians and sometimes will carry the name "Lughnasadh" for pagans; while wassail is a term used in older carols – we wassail our apple trees for a good harvest the next year.

Our agricultural year begins in November, putting the ewes to the ram and knowing that by the end of March the following year we will be lambing. Candlemas makes sense to me now as a theological act of solidarity in a way that I wouldn't have understood in the past. Our neighbour is lambing two months earlier than us, in the dark, needing a candle in the window for company. There is a deep loneliness in shepherding in the dark, waiting to help bring lambs to birth. It is also a time of deep wonder if, as we do, you lamb out in the field under the stars or in the pouring rain. New life in lambs and Easter usually coincide for us, but nothing is easy or guaranteed in this life process and there is tragedy as well as delight in it, as there is in the Holy Week story. Shearing in midsummer, haymaking at the same sort of time depending on the weather, ducklings hatching, lambs and piglets growing – all make that long green season of Trinity make sense to me. Then comes Lammas, harvest-loaf time, on the first of August, followed by Michaelmas at the end of September, before which you have to have finished picking blackberries or "the witches will spit on them", then Halloween and the struggle between good and evil. All of these speak of a responsiveness to the earth and the seasons as we experience them in the north, of a thanksgiving to the one who provides and to whom we return, a recognition that there are times of the year that are "thin", where heaven and earth are just a breath apart and we are held with "angels and archangels and the whole company of heaven".

Being tied to the agricultural seasons as a smallholder brings me back to the liturgical seasons of my childhood exposure to Anglicanism, firstly through primary school and then a village church choir and later other choirs. The rhythm and roundedness of both cycles weave together seasonal living, seasonal eating and seasonal praying. I'm not a big churchgoer any more, though as a retired priest I do help out when needed. Rather, the joy of the seasons as an Anglican for me is the learning to live with the seasons, without having to anticipate the next-but-one season's study course or services rota. Instead, anticipation is the proper preparation of planting seeds, booking the visiting ram, setting the eggs in the incubator and noting the date so we know when to stop turning them ready for hatching. That is not really preparation, but rather a part of the process of living seasonally. Now at last I can live in what seems like a more integrated way, acknowledging that when others nearby celebrate a pagan festival on the same day that I celebrate a Christian festival, we are connected by sun and moon, the stars and our hopes and fears, our awareness of the dead and our celebration of new life. As a parish priest I've always had an awareness of the other faith traditions and their special times, but now it is with those who cherish the earth that I can feel some kindred in this joy in the seasons, and I've begun to learn about how connected we are historically.

The cycle of liturgical seasons relates closely to the sabbath – the time of ceasing from work, from getting and having, from striving and wanting, and letting be for a time. What stops the working week being an endless round and the year being an unrelenting cycle is the genius of sabbath, learned from the Hebrew scriptures. Sabbath allows one to shed a protective layer and live joyfully with those around, and is a regular and repeatable occurrence. It teaches that such sabbath rest as I can achieve should not lead to others working without rest; that there is a forward movement from sabbath to a deeper justice between rich and poor; and that God's commanding intention is that we should honour that intention regularly and reliably. It teaches that sabbath is about joy, gift, worship, communion and community; that there is no scarcity of God's goodness; and that we do not have to struggle to secure our own lives.

Many of these things cannot be done by any individual by themselves but have an essential community dimension, much like being Jewish. Here we are making a life choice rather than a lifestyle choice. In choosing to acknowledge the seasons of the Church we are making a similar and connected choice – to acknowledge that all times are not the same, that God's blessings come in "due season", that the story of the life of Jesus and the founding of the Church gives us a rhythm to live by and a lectionary to read from, to save us from neglecting uncomfortable passages and sticking only to what we like.

Living seasonally has liturgical, agricultural and ethical dimensions. Praying and worshipping seasonally gives breadth to our thinking and longing. We use different psalms, different types of psalm chants, additional canticles, a deeper set of readings for each day, and not just Sunday, and a set of intentions for prayer that reflect where we are in the great story of God and humanity.

Living in the agricultural season rather than the supermarket lack of season means enjoying the fruits in their season, rather than strawberries in December and asparagus in August. There is a discipline to working seasonally, with the light, that means that not all seasons are the same, that the daylight is short at times and so very long at others, which gives different work in different months. For example, haymaking has to have four dry days in a row to allow cutting, turning and baling, and recently these days haven't been available at the right time and so hay, a staple crop, can't be made. Climate change is changing the agricultural seasons and we are beginning to notice it even at the very local level.

The ethical dimension of living seasonally rather than treating all times as the same relates to the previous agricultural issue. Climate change will affect us all, farmers and non-farmers alike. Wet summers and warmer winters in Britain will determine what grows and what fails, what kinds of animals to keep and the price of locally grown food. Climate change also affects the rest of the world, in particular those countries whose marginal land, which once produced food, is lost to desertification or flooding. To expect to get our unseasonable fruit and vegetables from such places in exchange for money when their real need is to grow food for themselves has real ethical questions attached to it, because people can't eat money.

It is in thinking about the joy of the seasons for this Anglican that such questions arise. For me it is no good simply wearing the liturgical colours of the season in the Eucharist without being deeply aware what the weather is like outside, what my farming neighbours are doing and what my lifestyle means for other people I will never meet but who produce the food I eat, the fibres of the clothes I wear and the fuel that allows me to travel, heat my home and cook the food I choose. Living without consideration – using electricity, gas and oil to keep me warm and travelling without understanding that they are finite resources, buying food without considering what might be a fair price for the grower and producer and what the welfare of the animal might be – is a way of life that now seems theologically untenable.

The seasons of the Anglican Communion could have taught me much of that, had I paid attention before, but there is now no escaping it. The lesson is the same as that of the sabbath. We are not a people worshipping the God of scarcity but the God of abundance who gives us "food in due season" (Psalm 145:15), so that we don't need to hoard and scramble to care for our isolated selves, but can follow the rhythm of the life of Jesus and the founding of the Church. Because of this, we can celebrate the saints and martyrs, live ethically and thoughtfully, know our deep connection with land and nature and share these insights with those from other faiths or understanding. It has taken me time to know my place in this scheme of things but I'm still learning and am joyful in it. Ecclesiastes 3:1-8 is of course the classic text for this way of living the seasons with joy:

For everything there is a season, and a time for every matter under heaven: a time to be born, and a time to die; a time to plant, and a time to pluck up what is planted; a time to kill, and a time to heal; a time to break down, and a time to build up; a time to weep, and a time to laugh; a time to mourn, and a time to dance; a time to throw away stones, and a time to gather stones together; a time to embrace, and a time to refrain from embracing; a time to seek, and a time to lose; a time to keep, and a time to throw away; a time to tear, and a time to sew; a time to keep silence, and a time to speak; a time to love, and a time to hate; a time for war, and a time for peace.

The Joy of English Church Buildings for an Anglican

by Gillian Cooper

Gillian is a lifelong Anglican who has worked within the Church of England as a priest, as a theological educator, in a cathedral and a diocesan office. Having experienced and led worship in a range of urban and village churches and a city-centre cathedral, she has developed an appreciation for church buildings of all varieties. She has been a regular Redemptorist Publications contributor since 2004.

I am eight years old, and I am in the car with my parents and four-year old sister. We are travelling from our village to Lincoln on a shopping trip. We compete to see who can catch the first glimpse of the cathedral. Suddenly, there it is, rising high above the flat countryside, its towers reaching up to heaven. It makes me feel small, but it is also familiar, a landmark of home.

Fifty years later, I am on the train, heading home after a day at work in Lincoln. And there it is again, floodlit in the dusk, still towering over the city. Now I understand the immense commitment that was needed to build it, and marvel at how important it must have been for so much time, money and effort to have been invested in it. In it, I see a symbol of the dominance of the Church of England in English life and culture, now less than it was, but in some measure still enduring despite the changes in our way of life.

Not far away from Lincoln Cathedral is a small village. Its church is tiny compared with the cathedral, but is still the highest building in the area, its tower clearly visible for miles around. Its regular congregation numbers a handful of people and the lack of money for its upkeep is painfully clear. The door creaks open and you are greeted by a smell of damp. On further inspection you can see that the tiled floor is cracked and the lighting needs an overhaul. Some years ago there was a suggestion that it should be closed, but it quickly became clear how much it mattered to the village community, whether they were churchgoers or not. The village without its church was unthinkable. Special services at Christmas and harvest time have always been well attended. Now there is a committee raising funds to renovate the church. There is talk of diversification. There are plans for a toddler group to meet there, and the possibility of opening a volunteer-run village shop in the vestry.

Not far away from that is another church. This one, built after the war, is on a housing estate. Some of the members of the congregation can remember it being built, at a time when new social housing was needed. The building is squat and functional but, like the village church, it too is loved by the community around it. Old photographs show the sixty-strong Sunday school getting on the bus for an outing to the coast, and vestments in the vestry are reminders of more "high Church" times past.

In his book *England's Thousand Best Churches*,[1] Simon Jenkins calls the churches he describes "a Museum of England". In them he finds an "experience not of faith, but rather of the memory of faith… witness to the bonds that have brought the English people together through a thousand years of history… It is through the churches of England that we learn who

---

1 Simon Jenkins, *England's Thousand Best Churches* (Harmondsworth: Penguin, 1999), xxvii-xxix.

we were and thus who we are and might become." Our churches are not only religious buildings. They are loved and respected by many who would not call themselves Christian, let alone Anglican.

Anglicans are no longer in the majority in England. "C of E" is no longer the default answer to official questions about religious affiliation. Church attendance numbers have plummeted, and despite the presence of Anglican bishops in the House of Lords, the Church of England seems increasingly irrelevant in society. Yet its buildings tell another story. They support the English longing for permanence, our sense of belonging in our land, and our need to feel part of a larger story. They are very visible reminders of a way of life for which we feel a certain nostalgia. But they also say something about the spiritual, about a dimension beyond the everyday, for which we are all searching.

Part of the joy of England's parish churches and cathedrals is that they are not exclusively Anglican. Their story begins at a time when Christianity in the British Isles was establishing itself as the true faith in opposition to paganism. Pagan shrines were taken over or replaced to ensure that the Christian Church presided over all aspects of local life, from birth to death. At the centre of each location the church building provided a focus for the newly Christian peoples, a worship place and a gathering place, a community hub.

At first church buildings were simple structures – an open space for trade as well as worship, an altar for celebrating the Mass, a tower for defence. The Norman conquest ushered in a new style of church building, one we still see in many of our churches today. The church building was in the shape of a cross, and carved stonework appeared. Churches began to be not just meeting places, but buildings that themselves communicated the faith they served through their decoration. Doom paintings terrified worshippers with visions of hell, their destination if they did not heed the Church's warnings and avoid sin. Carvings in the stonework showed saints and apostles, and in some places "green men", once venerated by pagan worship but now sanctified by their place in a Christian church. Much later stained glass was introduced, its design telling stories from the Bible and Christian tradition for people who were not necessarily literate. In time copies of the Ten Commandments appeared, and tombs and memorials provided reminders of mortality and encouraged the living of a good life. Angels gazed down from heavenly roofs, and crucifixes bore witness to the central tenets of the faith.

Churches also changed with theology and religious practice. Screens of wood or stone were built to separate the congregation from the place where the holiest rites were performed. Belfries were added so that the faithful could be called to prayer. The Reformation saw the destruction of much ornamentation and the introduction of more pews, so that congregations could sit while they listened to the sermons that became the most important element of churchgoing. In the Victorian period the success of the Anglo-Catholic Oxford Movement prompted church restoration and building in a Gothic style typified by the use of dark carved wood. More recently, churches have paid attention to the importance of fellowship and church buildings have become more flexible, with chairs replacing pews and seating arrangements that bring priest and people closer together and enable worshippers to interact with one another.

The glory of England's churches is in this change and variety. They tell the story of the Christian faith that became Anglicanism in this land. They show how down the ages our understanding of faith has changed, and how the place of the Church in the community has developed. Elements from different times tell us of weddings conducted in porches, of the holiness of the sanctuary area, of valiant knights memorialised in stone, of religious fervour encouraged by fear of death and hell, of ancestors who lived and died within earshot of the bells. We can often trace the story of a place by the styles of architecture and decoration that have been laid over one another down the years.

I imagine there will be some incumbents and churchwardens who will raise their eyebrows at the title of this chapter as they struggle with the huge cost and effort of repairing, maintaining, developing and insuring these difficult buildings. Simon Jenkins believes that the wider community will need to take over some of the responsibility for the care of churches if they are to survive.[2] As numbers of churchgoers diminish, buildings can seem like millstones around the necks of worshipping communities, using up precious time and resources that could be better spent on outreach and service. If the state wants to hold on to the nation's Christian heritage, it may indeed have to do more to preserve its buildings beyond the current level of grant funding.

Some would argue that the Anglican Communion no longer needs church buildings. For people of faith, there is always some discomfort about the

---

2 Jenkins, *England's Thousand Best Churches*, xxviii.

need for buildings, as the Bible illustrates. The Old Testament writers show an ambivalence in this area. The Temple in Jerusalem is the place where God is most obviously encountered. Its importance is emphasised by the detailed instructions for its construction, placed in the context of the foundation story of the exodus and wilderness wanderings. It is celebrated in the Psalms:

> How lovely is your dwelling place, O Lord of hosts! My soul longs, indeed it faints for the courts of the Lord.
>
> Psalm 84:1-2

Yet at the heart of the Temple is the Ark of the Covenant, a portable sign of the presence of God, carried with God's people on the move. It is the people, and their relationship with God, that are at the heart of faith, not the building, for all its glory. The early Christians met in homes, without initially feeling a need for a special building. It is perhaps the human desire for stability and need for structure that attempts to contain faith in a building. We feel more secure when we can go to a special place to meet God, rather than allowing God into the whole of our lives. Perhaps without buildings we would find freedom to allow God to lead us into new ways of being Christian.

Today there are many alternative places where Christians can meet for worship and fellowship. The work of mission and ministry involves going out into the community, rather than always inviting people in. A congregation's focus on the needs of the building can easily become a distraction from the prayer and action which is the essence of Christian faith. It could be argued that ancient buildings should be abandoned by the Church of England and left for the state to rescue as heritage sites, or to decay into picturesque ruins, so that the Church can concentrate on preaching the Gospel.

It is, however, significant that there is an extreme reluctance to close churches. Those that no longer have congregations and fall out of use are nevertheless preserved. The work of the Churches Conservation Trust protects and keeps open churches that the Church of England can no longer maintain, not merely as romantic ruins, but as places that become available to their communities in new and creative ways. Why do we want church buildings so much that we are prepared to go to such lengths to keep them, even when we no longer need them for their original purpose?

There has been a resurgence of interest in discovering our family history, as witness the success of the television series *Who Do You Think You Are?* Churches hold baptism, marriage and burial records. They may no longer be in the physical church building, but they tell of life's significant moments marked in a particular place. Standing in that place, we can imagine our ancestors and feel closer to them. Sometimes their names may appear on ledger stones in the graveyard, on wall memorials or on brasses set into the floor.

The story of a community can be discovered too. Social history can be traced through the occupations of those who have lived in a particular place, and marks of events in British history can be discovered. Perhaps one of the most moving churches in the country is in the village of Eyam in Derbyshire, where parish records celebrate the courage of the parish priest and people of the village in 1665 at the time of the Great Plague, as they shut themselves in to prevent the spread of infection. Nearly 280 of the 350 villagers died, including the priest's wife and small son. In other places, laid-up military standards tell of a community's involvement in war, and prompt reflection about the responsibilities of those who follow the Prince of Peace. The nation's history is remembered at special services such as Remembrance Sunday. Occasions such as the harvest festival and the beating of the bounds celebrate a way of life that has changed significantly but is still valued. At Christmas, churches are full of people singing carols that, despite their secular origins, have been preserved by the churches. Cathedrals hold the corporate memories of the cities in which they are set, as civic life has been marked by church ceremonies down the ages.

Beyond all this, however, the church buildings themselves seem to have a role to play. Walkers may call into a village church for a quiet sit down. Shoppers enter a city-centre cathedral to light a candle and escape for a moment from the commercial bustle outside. People of other faiths or none seem to find in church buildings a peace and stillness that they value, whatever the age of the church. There is a sense of otherness, of holiness even, about these places, as if prayers are embedded in their stones.

That is not to say that the heritage of churches should be preserved at the expense of their use. Church buildings need to continue to change and adapt, as they always have. They are still places of worship, and ways of worshipping continue to change as they have down the centuries. For example, many church councils have discovered how hard it is to get permission to remove pews. Fine examples of Victorian woodwork are defended by heritage societies, and rightly so. Yet there is a case for removing them to create a more flexible space in which to hold worship that meets the needs of today's churchgoers, and that also opens up the possibility of other uses. Many churches and cathedrals are returning to the original pattern, at the very beginnings of Christianity in England, where the church is the community hub, providing space for schools and playgroups, shops and studios, concerts and parties. Some are offered for the use of other denominations, and even other faiths. They are finding their contemporary place in the communities they serve, not as historical monuments but as living, breathing spaces where people may meet one another, and meet God.

It may be that our church buildings in all their wonderful variety are still something the Church of England can offer to our nation. The buildings themselves preach the Gospel in ways we do not always realise or understand. We look after them not for ourselves, but for others. They tell people about history and about faith. At the heart of every community they bear witness to the existence of a dimension beyond physical existence, and to the possibility of communication with the divine. They are sacred places, where God may be encountered by anyone who enters. Simply by being there, they embody the presence of God.

As a lifelong Anglican, I have experienced many churches. I have sat under leaking roofs, had to keep my gloves on, and competed with the noise of traffic and commerce outside. I have enjoyed carefully designed lighting, and the light of candles in the absence of electricity. I have gazed at pictures in stained glass, and at the light shining through old clear glass onto uneven stone floors. I have been inspired time and again by the commitment and love of local people for their church or cathedral. I have worked and worshipped in cathedrals, modern housing estate churches, ancient village churches, and prosperous suburban churches. None of them has failed to bring me joy.

The Joy of the Liturgy for an Anglican

by the Revd Canon Simon Cowling

Simon has been Rector of Bolton Abbey in the Diocese of Leeds since 2013. Since his ordination in 1991 he has held posts in the inner city, in the suburbs, and in the countryside in both parish and cathedral contexts. This has given him considerable insight into the glorious diversity of the Church of England and a keen appreciation of the opportunities and challenges it faces in engaging with contemporary culture. Simon has a particular interest in the relationship between worship, mission and church buildings, and currently serves as chair of the Leeds Diocesan Advisory Committee. He is married to Anne and they have three adult children.

Fifty years ago most parish churches, especially in towns, were still able to muster a robed choir of men and boys. Such a choir provided me, as a six-year-old, with a front-row introduction to the liturgy of the Church of England. Even now, I remember the thrill of sitting in the choir stalls and being able to watch the liturgical action close up. I also remember being introduced to a new and excitingly mysterious register of language which, in the case of hymns, became so inextricably linked with music that after a few years as a choirboy it became impossible to think of the one without the other. So, for instance, like many cradle Anglicans, I find it difficult to read George Herbert's poem "Antiphon (I)" without the fine tune, Luckington, that Basil Harwood wrote for it over two hundred and fifty years later:

Chorus
    Let all the world in ev'ry corner sing,
    "My God and King."

Verse
    The heav'ns are not too high,
    His praise may thither flie:
    The earth is not too low,
    His praises there may grow.

Chorus
    Let all the world in ev'ry corner sing,
    "My God and King."

Verse
    The church with psalms must shout,
    No doore can keep them out:
    But above all, the heart
    Must bear the longest part.

Chorus
    Let all the world in ev'ry corner sing,
    "My God and King."

In his book of practical advice to the clergy, *A Priest to the Temple*, George Herbert writes that:

> (the) Countrey Parson, when he is to read divine services, composeth himselfe to all possible reverence; lifting up his heart and hands, and eyes, and using all other gestures which may expresse a hearty, and unfeyned devotion.[1]

---

1 George Herbert, *A Priest to the Temple* (1652), 17-20.

With a reticence that is at the same time beguiling and frustrating, Herbert leaves it to the reader to infer what these "other gestures" might be, and how the congregation might respond to such gestures. Happily, though, he has left us something rather less allusive in "Antiphon (I)". John Drury has written that in this poem "[a] country congregation is imagined, bellowing its psalms… and audible in the fields beyond its door":[2] the congregation answers the priest's four-line versicles with bursts of praise that fly, grow, and penetrate the heaviest wooden door, perhaps taking their lead from the bodily gestures that Herbert describes in *A Priest to the Temple*. Maybe Herbert has his own Bemerton congregation in mind, but his poem will surely resonate with anyone who has sung a congregational hymn or worship song with any degree of enthusiasm. Such singing must fully engage not only the congregation's souls but also its bodies.

Taken together, these snippets of Herbert's prose and verse evoke a spirituality that is suffused by a deep joy, both spiritual and physical. Such a joy seems at first glance to be at some distance from the sober ethos of the Book of Common Prayer. Here were to be found the only legally permitted services of the seventeenth-century Church of England into which George Herbert was ordained. Yet it is a joy that we find time and again in Herbert's writing. It is the same joy that many generations of Church of England congregations, in city and suburb as well as countryside, have found (though they might have sometimes had to search hard to find it) in celebrating corporately the liturgies of the Book of Common Prayer. And it is the same joy that such congregations have also found in the many other liturgies, derived ultimately from the Book of Common Prayer, that have proliferated in glorious diversity both in the Church of England and across the provinces of the Anglican Communion in the past few decades. Before turning our attention to the journey that has led to this diversity, we first explore what we mean when we speak of "liturgy".

Liturgy is worship (and vice versa)

There is an old, and to my mind not very funny joke that runs like this:

Q. What is the difference between a liturgist and a terrorist?
A. You can negotiate with a terrorist.

Terrorism, of course, is not a humorous subject. But leaving that aside, the joke depends on a simplistic and rather outdated understanding of both liturgists and liturgy. It suggests a value-laden distinction between *liturgy* and *worship*. Those who are interested in liturgy are viewed as, at best,

---

2 John Drury, *Music at Midnight: The Life and Poetry of George Herbert* (London: Allen Lane, 2013).

rather eccentric; at worst, as completely inflexible. In contrast, worship is the province of those who have dispensed with liturgy. Unshackled from liturgy's burdensome restrictions on the activity of the Holy Spirit, they are able freely to offer their worship in body, mind and spirit. The Liturgical Commission of the Church of England was alive to the dangers of this distinction in its 2007 report *Transforming Worship*:

> It will be helpful to keep the term *liturgy* free from connotations of formality or church style, as if it were a starchier or high-church synonym for *worship*. Liturgies are much more than texts: although words are an important part of liturgy, so too are movement and silence and music, and the way in which they are all articulated in space.[3]

Nevertheless, though in a less value-laden way, the report chooses to continue to distinguish between liturgy and worship:

> If worship is the deepest response of redeemed humankind to God's loving purpose, then liturgy is the set of particular structured actions in which worship is expressed and by which worship is released. Liturgy is the occasion of worship.[4]

I am not sure that even this distinction is fair – or even theologically sound. It characterises liturgy as a kind of handmaid for worship. It assumes that worship is constituted by the flesh, sinews and breath ("the deepest response of redeemed humankind") which clothe and animate the dry bones ("the particular structured actions") of liturgy.

The word "liturgy" derives from the ancient Greek words *leitos*[5] (belonging to the people) and *ergon* (work). In ancient Athens a liturgy was a public function performed by wealthy citizens. Such liturgies might include funding the performance of dramas at annual festivals or the provision of a banquet at such festivals. In other words, a liturgy was a public work undertaken by wealthy citizens for the good of, and on behalf of, the whole people. This sense of a liturgy as something done on behalf of others is reflected in the books of the New Testament, where it acquires a more theological meaning. The Jewish people at the time of Jesus Christ understood those who served as priests in the Jerusalem Temple to be intermediaries, offering sacrifices and burning incense on behalf of the whole people of God. Thus Luke describes how the

---

3 Liturgical Commission of the Church of England, *Transforming Worship: Living the New Creation* (London: Liturgical Commission, 2007).
4 *Transforming Worship.*
5 In classical Greek this adjective, derived from the noun *laos* ("people"), is found only in the compound word *leitourgia* ("liturgy").

priest Zechariah, the father of John the Baptist, returns home "when his time of *service* [Greek: 'liturgy'] was ended" (Luke 1:23). But the writer of the Letter to the Hebrews takes the theology into new territory altogether. We are now to understand Christ's offering of himself as a "liturgy" in the fullest sense: the "merciful and faithful high priest" (Hebrews 2:17) gives his own life on behalf of the whole world in order that he might be "the mediator of a better covenant" (Hebrews 8:6). Redeemed humankind's response of penitence, prayer and praise to our great high priest's own "more excellent *ministry*" (Greek: "liturgy", Hebrews 8:6) requires us to collapse the distinction between worship and liturgy altogether. Our worship *is* our liturgy and our liturgy *is* our worship – an insight reflected in Thomas Cranmer's Prayer of Oblation, now said by the priest after Communion in the 1662 version of the Book of Common Prayer:

> O Lord and heavenly Father, we thy humble servants entirely desire thy fatherly goodness mercifully to accept this our sacrifice of praise and thanksgiving… [and] here we offer and present unto thee, O Lord, ourselves, our souls and bodies, to be a reasonable, holy and lively sacrifice unto thee.

Nearly a century before George Herbert's poems were published, Cranmer's prose speaks of worship as an offering both spiritual and physical – a ministry, a liturgy, that is made prayerfully and joyfully by the Church on behalf of the world it serves in response to Christ's self-offering.

Cranmer and Common Prayer

> And whereas heretofore there hath been great diversity in saying and singing in Churches within this Realm; some following *Salisbury* Use, some *Hereford* Use, and some the Use of *Bangor*, some of *York*, some of *Lincoln*; now from henceforth all the whole Realm shall have but one Use.[6]

It is clear from this single sentence that Thomas Cranmer took a rather dim view of diversity. In introducing "one Use" for the whole of Edward VI's realm within his single volume 1549 Book of Common Prayer, Cranmer's intention was both to reduce the confusion caused by the liturgical variation found in the various "uses" he lists, and equally to reduce the confusion caused by the complexity of the elaborate rules that had developed to determine which liturgical texts should be read on any particular occasion. He writes with a dry wit, and obvious frustration,

---

6 Preface to the First Prayer Book of Edward VI, 1549.

of the medieval liturgies his prayer book was to replace: "many times there was more business to find out what should be read than to read it when it was found out".[7] Cranmer's 1549 Book of Common Prayer, and its 1552 successor, established the principle of a uniform liturgical practice, "common prayer", in the Church of England that has, theoretically at least, survived to this day. The 1662 version of the Book of Common Prayer, introduced after the Commonwealth period, remains the normative liturgical text for the Church of England as well as the source of much of its official doctrine.

This is not the place to rehearse the twists and turns of liturgical reform and renewal in the Church of England over the past century. The Royal Commission of 1906 reported that the provisions for worship in the 1662 Book of Common Prayer were "too narrow for the religious life of the present generation". Sufficient to say that between its findings and the publication of Common Worship, much ink (though, at least to my knowledge, no blood) has been spilt in successive attempts to arrive at a set of liturgies that will do justice both to Cranmer's wish for "one Use", and offer liturgies that are appropriate to the missional and pastoral needs of our times.

On the making of many books – the joy of diversity (Ecclesiastes 12:12)

Given Cranmer's misgivings about the complicated liturgies of the medieval Church, it might be thought ironic that the Church of England's most recent liturgical reforms have resulted in multiple volumes of services. To the uninitiated, the complexity of this expansive liturgical provision surely equals that of the pre-Reformation liturgies that Cranmer was seeking to replace.[8] Looked at from another point of view, however, the rich variety of services in Common Worship provides a renewed opportunity for Church of England congregations to offer worship, to engage joyfully in liturgy properly understood, in which words, music, silence, movement, colour, space and human senses all combine. Such worship both reflects and begets a twenty-first-century equivalent of George Herbert's "hearty, and unfeyned devotion". The provision of Common Worship also demonstrates, in its flexibility and variety, an awareness of the increasingly diverse cultures into which the Church of England must speak if it is to continue to fulfil its historic mission to be a Church for the whole nation.

---

7 Preface to the First Prayer Book of Edward VI, 1549.
8 For a thoughtful discussion on the supposed complexity of *Common Worship* see chapter 1 of Mark Earey, *Beyond Common Worship: Anglican Identity and Liturgical Diversity* (London: SCM, 2013).

One significant feature of Common Worship has been the formal reintroduction into the authorised services of the Church of England of what are called "sacramentals". These are the material objects used in worship that help people to reflect on the wider significance of what they are doing. An example of such a sacramental is a palm cross. The pre-Reformation Palm Sunday procession marked the beginning of Holy Week. The triumphal entry of Christ into Jerusalem a few days before his crucifixion was re-enacted in virtually every community. Clergy and laity, carrying branches representing palms, gathered in the open air; the palms were blessed and the procession moved joyfully into church. Sacramentals such as palms (and indeed processions themselves) were abolished at the Reformation in England because they were thought to encourage superstition. The collect and readings for Cranmer's Sunday next before Easter contain no reference at all to the events surrounding Jesus' entry into Jerusalem. By providing an authorised service[9] in which palm crosses are used as a reminder of Christ's death and resurrection the Church of England is connecting, in a small but important way, with a contemporary culture in which physical manifestations of deeply held feelings (such as the now ubiquitous appearance of flowers where roadside fatalities have taken place) have assumed an importance that would have been inconceivable even two generations ago. Other sacramentals commended in Common Worship include the use of ashes on Ash Wednesday, and the use of holy oil for baptism and confirmation, both of which also disappeared at the Reformation in England but which are now routinely used and widely welcomed by Church of England congregations as an enrichment of their worship and as a tangible reminder of the materiality of God's creation.

Only connect

Over twenty-five years ago Rowan Williams summed up what he saw as the specifically Anglican contribution to liturgy: "[It] has to do with the making of liturgy that connects the catholic pattern of life in the Body of Christ with the patterns of community that prevail in *this* place and time."[10]

This remark could not have been made in the nineteenth century. It took a long time for any thoroughgoing liturgical revision to take place in the Church of England after 1662. But, in the twentieth and twenty-first centuries at least, the Church has shown an increasingly creative response to, and awareness of, the rapid shifts in the social and cultural context in

---

9 "The Liturgy of Palm Sunday", in *Common Worship: Times and Seasons* (London: Church House, 2006).
10 Rowan Williams, "Imagining the Kingdom", in Kenneth Stevenson and Bryan Spinks (eds), *The Identity of Anglican Worship* (London: Mowbray, 1991).

which it operates. Part of this context is one of increased individualism, of a need for self-fulfilment that transcends the apparently fixed certainties of the society from which the Book of Common Prayer emerged. It is vanishingly unlikely that society will ever again know such fixed certainties. But in and through its worship the Church of England offers a reminder that, amidst all that might separate us, there is still great joy to be found in "doing liturgy" together; in offering worship to God that engages us in body, soul and spirit; and in doing so in a way that connects what we understand of God's ways with the world with how we understand the gloriously messy materiality of that world. That is something that George Herbert, with whom we began, fully understood. We leave the last word to another poet, the American Mark Jarman, who also understands this connectedness. In the first few lines of one of his "Unholy Sonnets" he connects us also with one of the foundational texts of Anglican liturgy: Thomas Cranmer's Book of Common Prayer Collect for Purity:

> Almighty God, to you all hearts are open,
> All throats, all voice boxes, all inner ears,
> All pupils, all tear ducts, all cavities
> Inside the skull inside the trick of flesh.[11]

As I look back, I would characterise my early attraction to liturgical worship as primarily aesthetic – colour, music, movement and vestments all combining to instil in a small boy a deep sense of the otherness of worship, yet an otherness in which (paradoxically perhaps) I was able to participate. And it was precisely this sense of otherness combined with participation that drew me back to the Church as a young adult and set me on the path to eventual ordination. To paraphrase R. S. Thomas, liturgy had brought me to the borders of my understanding, and God had called me, and continues to call me, onward.[12]

---

11 Mark Jarman, "Unholy Sonnet 9", in *Questions for Ecclesiastes* (Ashland, OR: Story Line Press, 1997).
12 See "Gradual", in R. S. Thomas, *Collected Poems 1945-1990* (London: Phoenix Press, 1995).

The Joy of Laughter for an Anglican

by Paul Kerensa

Paul is a stand-up comedian, comedy scriptwriter and author of several books including *Hark! The Biography of Christmas, So a Comedian Walks into a Church* and *Genesis: The Bibluffer's Guide.* As a stand-up, he won ITV's Take the Mike award and was a finalist in the BBC New Comedy Awards. He's a member of the British Comedy Awards Academy, as one of the award-winning writers of BBC1's *Miranda.* His other writing credits include *Not Going Out, Top Gear* and Channel 4's *TFI Friday* revival, as well as radio such as *Dead Ringers, The Now Show* and *The News Quiz.* He's also a regular broadcaster for the Pause for Thought slot on Chris Evans' Radio 2 Breakfast Show. Paul is married with two young children and likes the band Roxette a little too much.

A month of Sundays…

Dear Diary,
As a church-hopping comedian on the road – a kneel-down stand-up –
I've been lately been pondering the Anglican sense of humour. Others
can ponder our sense of purpose, or sense of faith, or (in one church I've
visited recently) sense of smell. But the last four Sundays have seen me
walk into a bar, generally cross a few roads, and knock knock on a few
doors. So let's see if the joke's on me…

SUNDAY 1: SO THE VICAR SAID…

"The Lord be with you," the vicar usually says.

"And also with you," comes the congregation's reply.

Except on this occasion the vicar's microphone wasn't working. He tapped
it, and muttered off to the side: "There's something wrong with the mic."

The congregation replied instinctively, "And also with you."

It's not known how many responded on auto-pilot, and how many were
knowingly in on the joke.

It's an old story – and of course didn't happen today in my church. It's the
stuff of legends, though I did once meet a preacher who claimed to have
been that original mic-suffering minister in the joke. I still don't know
whether to believe him or not. It's like meeting the original Englishman,
Irishman and Scotsman. Even if they were accompanied by a horse with a
long face, you still wouldn't believe that it's them.

Jokes can be diverting, entertaining, joy-bringing parables. To focus on
the historicity of a joke's plot is to miss the point – like asking what the
Prodigal Son's name was, or whether that plank got in someone's eye due to
an accident in the workplace (in which case they could make a claim if they
called a helpline).

Today's church service included giggles at lighter mishaps. A child leant
on the organ during the notices (I think some of the worship group
were surprised we even had an organ). Oh, and the vicar's PowerPoint
presentation went rogue, racing through images like a flicker-book.

"That was a quicker sermon than I'd planned," he quipped. "I'm sorry to say
that it's longer than that."

There's a Yiddish proverb: "Man plans, and God laughs." So perhaps when those plans don't work out, we're just joining in with the divine chuckles. In the formal institution of the Church, laughs are only heightened as we try so hard to keep everything in its place. Anglicanism's own flavour of faith is historically very ordered, so unplanned *dis*order is all the more noticeable. I see the Church as man-made but God-blessed. So I imagine our creator – the setup to our punchline – looking down through almighty fingers as we humbly attempt worship.

"Oh, you're going to let children near the organ, are you? Using PowerPoint in your sermon? Good luck with that..." God loves a trier, and we can be very trying.

Today's service had its fair sure of planned humour, too. Jokes are often near the top of a preacher's toolbox – handy for easing the tone, before employing the heftier tools underneath. Occasionally the joke's even on topic. In fact when it's not, we get one of my favourite preacher tools, the crowbar, over-forcing the joke to fit the sermon.

"... So the kid said to the priest, 'It's okay – the sign says that God's watching the doughnuts!' And you know, I think in many ways, the Ten Commandments are like doughnuts..."

Our vicar is more careful. His stories are true, from his own past, and normally self-deprecating. We laugh with him, empathetically – there but for the grace of God go I. The polar opposite is a preacher I once saw who poached a good shaggy dog story he'd heard from an American speaker, about his dog. He went on to tell the same story at his own church, as if it was his own. The congregation were baffled – they knew their minister didn't have a dog, nor a ranch in Texas. I fear the point was lost that day, especially if the sermon was about honesty.

No, the stories we warm to are less exotic, humbler fare. The Anglican character – at least from where I stand, sit and kneel in this corner of the Church of England – is tied to centuries of Englishness, to a quiet resilience that's seen off crisis after crisis. This kind of Anglicanism is like its own supreme governor, our monarch. We are not brash, we like a cup of tea, and we like an underdog (maybe even an under-corgi). As home to the nation's weddings and funerals, Anglicanism gravitates to the middle ground, to welcome all-comers.

As Eddie Izzard noted in one of his stand-up routines, we come from such a comfortable base that an Anglican inquisition would be "Cake or death?"

"Oh, I'll have the cake please..."

Our sense of humour is mainstream. We're a broad Church, catering to all – from the crèche to the pensioners' lunch club. We'll take Pam Ayres over Frankie Boyle, and prefer light observational comedy to anything too satirical or controversial. Laughter may be a God-given joy, but comedy revels in disorder. Church is ordered and structured – so a little disorder goes a long way.

I find services like today's enormously anchoring. The reliability of my home church, that's been here centuries. I can go and work in Orpington, Orkney or Auckland, and come back to the same smiling faces here, as well as the odd non-smiling one, who thought the toddler should have been kept well away from the organ. Even then, a wry smile was cracked to the vicar over post-service coffee: "I told you we should never have got PowerPoint."

SUNDAY 2: SO THERE WAS THIS CHURCH OFF THE M1...

Some weeks, I'm a nomadic churchgoer – and sometimes I veer from my roots. Any building with a cross on top, I'll walk in. It might be C of E, it might be C of something else, or occasionally it's a pharmacy.

Today's church, far enough north that the M1 had just run out, was a glimmering new-build. I assumed C of Something Else, but no, this was Anglican in modern clothing – no red brick in sight, just brilliant white, outside and in. The wood laminate flooring hinted that it wanted to look classic, claiming some of the history, while also being wipe-clean for toddler group. Ikea don't do churches, but if they did...

The notice board told of ballet classes, Narcotics Anonymous and NCT meetings (presumably not all at the same time). This church has put its flag in the ground as the hub of the community – not just for weddings, funerals and bar mitzvahs (all right, not many bar mitzvahs), but also for birthday parties and extracurricular shenanigans. Perhaps in an age where the high street is no longer the guaranteed centre of events, it's more important than ever for the Church to stake its claim as the local focal point.

As I entered for their morning worship there were a few glimmers of recognition. I'm not showing off – I was only there the night before doing a comedy show. Comedy? In a church? Well, yes. Half of my gigs lately have been in churches. There's a great demand for coming together and having a laugh as a community, as a church, as a bunch of friends and congregants and neighbours.

Last night, the minister looked out at the audience, wide-eyed and delighted: "I don't know half of these people!" he exclaimed. That meant that either lots of non-churchgoers had turned up, or he's got a very bad memory of his regular flock.

It was a fun show, though, as is often the case, I had to spend a couple of minutes helping them over the barrier of "Can we laugh in church?" We like to laugh, but we need a little reassurance about exactly when to – so some look to the vicar first. It can cause a three-second delay at some loftier churches, while they glance over for permission. (In some Pentecostal churches, they laugh three seconds early, just happy to be there. If I ever find a half-Anglican, half-Pentecostal audience, the laughs should average out about right.)

This morning, as Sunday service commenced, an elderly gent leaned over and told me that he had enjoyed the show, but you could hear the surprise in his voice – I think more surprise that there was a show at all, rather than surprise that he enjoyed it. And I wasn't surprised at his surprise. Anglicans love tradition, and turning a church building into a comedy club may not be an obvious choice. I've known churches to use their premises for community cinema, live music events, even wrestling nights. Then again, I know one Christian comic who contacted some American churches ahead of his holiday in the southern states, asking if any would consider hosting his church comedy show while he was passing. Some responded that they had their own in-house comedian – like a court jester – while others were at the stricter end of the spectrum: "How dare you even suggest using our altar as a den for your mockery!", read one. (I should note, I've never done a gig at the altar.) Once again, Anglicanism sits happily between the extremes.

Michelangelo has a lot to answer for. His Sistine Chapel was so good that arts in the Church peaked and stopped there for some time. Creativity has always been theoretically encouraged (after all, creating was one of the first things that God did), just in low doses. Christian art is inspirational, warm and encouraging, but not challenging. Modern art has largely yet to find a place in the Church – I can't see Tracey Emin's bed or Damien Hirst's sheep (even a lost one) doing a tour of cathedrals – though conceptual artwork of sculpture and installations have found a pew, where appropriate.

"Appropriate." Maybe that's the key. The comedy shows we bring to churches are careful to keep the tone and content welcoming, open and indeed, "appropriate". We all want to laugh together – "with", but not "at" – as a way of embracing God's creation.

Let's not forget that Jesus used humour. Granted it was no stand-up routine on the mount, but his observations used exaggerated concepts like planks in eyes to make a point. If it doesn't sound laugh-out-loud funny now, then read a Shakespeare comedy – five hundred years on, and the humour is tricky to perceive on first reading. The Gospels are four times as old as Shakespeare's plays. Tastes change. One thing that doesn't, though, is that we all like a joke, even in church. Sometimes we just need to be told that it's fine to laugh.

SUNDAY 3: SO THE COMEDIAN SAID TO THE VICAR, "WHY THE LONG FACE?"…

At last night's comedy club gig, there were four comedians, a hundred or so audients – and a vicar in the front row. He clearly felt out of place, though the gig was in an arts centre, not too rough and ready. And he could have kept a low profile of course, although I guess the thing about being a vicar is that when asked what you do for a living, you're not meant to lie. So when the compère challenged him, he had to confess.

"What do I do?" he cringed. "Nothing much."

She wasn't moving on, so after a pause he added: "I'm a vicar."

The audience ooed.

"Oh. Right," the compère said, stalling for time. "So Monday to Saturday, like you say – nothing much."

A light laugh, even though we knew he spends the week doing everything from funeral visits to, er… well I'm sure there are other things too.

"Where's your dog collar?"

"It's at home," joked the minister. "I share it with the dog."

Solid laugh from the crowd. The compère only now realised that her front row target was a professional public speaker.

"Why are vicars so funny?" she asked. "I mean funny peculiar, not funny ha-ha?"

I think the vicar took it personally. "Well, back in nineteenth-century literature, the vicar used to be the pretty sexy object of affection."

That was unexpected.

"You know, the young heroine lusting after the local parson. Then some roguish farmer comes along and beats the parson to it."

"To what? A pulp?"

"Yes, the literature was somewhat pulpish, you could say. As opposed to 'pulpit', which is what I stand in."

This was one droll deacon.

The blushing compère checked her watch. "Yeah, well you're not in one now, so kindly shut the…" She continued, rather bluely, to ask him to keep quiet – a bit harsh given that she started the conversation.

Perhaps the notion of the "comedy vicar" is a relative new invention. I grew up on a TV diet of *Monty Python*, *The Two Ronnies* and 1970s sitcoms. The Pythons threw on cassocks nearly as often as they threw on dresses; *To the Manor Born* and *Dad's Army* both featured God-botherers who were dithering community-botherers too. The bumbling Derek Nimmo of *All Gas and Gaiters* led to the bumbling Rowan Atkinson of *Four Weddings and a Funeral*. Any TV vicar of the nineties was either Dawn French or a corrupt (though rarely murderous) *Midsomer Murders* bit-part. Then came the self-analytical *Rev*, and at the time of writing, our televisual reverends are Kate Bottley and Richard Coles (I'm pretty sure Bottley and Coles is a shoe shop, or perhaps a solicitors').

The current TV rent-a-clergy are doing their bit to normalise Anglicanism. But for decades the Church of England has been an institution to be smirked at, more so than other flavours of faith – just because it's better known. In my capacity as an occasional comedy writer I've been in script meetings where a church was to be featured.

"How about we make it a Baptist church?" I suggested. Just for a change really. I couldn't tell you when I last saw a Baptist, Methodist or charismatic evangelical place of worship on the television.

"We'll keep it as is," said the producer, referring to the centuries-old Anglican building we'd currently picked out. "It's shorthand."

She had a point. It's self-fulfilling typecasting. Make it one of the other "shades of grace" and we'd have to explain to the audience what they're looking at. By the time they've worked out what a Vineyard church is, or realised that this isn't a conference centre but a church, they've missed the plot of the scene. And so it continues – the Church of England remains the media's favourite church, and sometimes the butt of the joke. I guess we don't mind. At least we're being talked about.

Equally, last night's priestly heckler didn't mind being part of the show. There was a spot of blushing, yes, but it's nearly Pentecost so red's the colour of the moment. I think the vicar enjoyed it. After all, he chose the front row, probably because it was only one step away from being on stage. The microphone was just out of reach – so let's be thankful for small mercies.

SUNDAY 4: SO THERE WAS THIS TODDLER…

I'm away with the family this weekend, in some rainy corner of the Chilterns. This morning, wife, toddler, pre-schooler and I visited a medieval church – new to us, if not to the parishioners, some of whom looked like they'd been at the cutting of the ribbon. It was high Church – smells, bells, hearing-aid yells and possibly a *Book of Kells* somewhere in the vestry.

Despite being the only children there, ours behaved very well. In fact our youngest lasted all the way 'til the sermon before emitting a sound. But what a sound it was.

As the minister said, "Before I begin, let us pray for God to speak through me today…" – right on cue, my eighteen-month-old broke the loudest of winds. A whiffy masterpiece resonated through the echoing heights of the ancient building, causing sniggers from a few, one loud guffaw, and a supportive smile from the churchwarden nearby that implied she'd been there. From most, though, there was a reverent silence and the odd disgruntled look.

You might ask why they didn't laugh. It was a perfectly timed, unfortunate, unplanned, innocent toddler emission! God created this child, and that marvellous trumping sound too. He created it loud and funny. Surely the human body – warts, farts and all – is a brilliantly beautiful hilarious walking piece of comedy all of its own.

Then again, perhaps it's best that they were not amused. Just as the vaulted ceiling amplified the rasp, the comic value was amplified too, simply *because* of those who disapproved. The loftier the institution, the higher the church, the greater the fall when comic moments knock sacred cows off their perches. (Let's gloss over the fact that cows don't sit on perches, but again, that's a funny image.)

This is the Church of the nation – the monarch heads it, archbishops oversee it, God smiles upon it and even smirks at our antics, I'm sure. So when this carefully ordered hierarchy is disrupted with a simple sound from my baby's bottom, I think it's allowably funny, in part because we try and restore order as quickly as possible.

Sometimes the organist starts again because he's played a bum note. The choir might have a tone-deaf chorister who doesn't know any better. The minister might mispronounce a name during the marriage vows. A toddler might herald the sermon with a downstairs fanfare. This is life, in all its unpredictable joy – and our Church hosts life's key moments. This backdrop of beautiful weddings, profound baptisms and sombre funerals only heightens the hilarity. There was a fall of man, but the pratfalls of man continue, and our stumbles cause the giggles. I think that God joins in with our laughter, because we're only human, and in Jesus, so was he once.

So Dear Diary,

God bless Anglicanism and its full range – from Messy Church to bells and smells (and apologies for when my toddler brings the smells).

It's a Church rooted in the past, but the future is gleefully unknown to us – so in the meantime we'll smile, as we unknowingly stroll towards life's banana skins.

Paul

The Joy of Poetry
for an Anglican

by the Revd Rachel Mann

Rachel is an Anglican parish priest, theologian and writer. She is poet-in-residence at Manchester Cathedral and is the author of four books, including the bestselling memoir of growing up transgender, *Dazzling Darkness*. Her latest book, *Fierce Imaginings*, examines the place of the Great War and Remembrance in post-Brexit Britain. Her poetry and criticism have appeared in a wide variety of academic and poetry journals as well as newsprint.

"There's blood between us, love, my love."

Christina Rossetti, "The Convent Threshold"

It may come as a shock to some readers, but I am not especially inspired by Christian poetry. In my mind, I associate – perhaps unfairly – the phrase with sickly, sentimental verse. Poetry is either good or bad, fine or inadequate. The qualifier "Christian" really adds little. And yet I am inclined to make an exception for the idea of Anglican poetry. I have been drawn to it again and again because of its wide and wonderful contribution to the English language itself.

For a tradition founded in political machination (indeed, a king's desire for a new bride), Anglicanism's richest and most distinctive joys might ultimately be found in words. Thankfully, not so much in its rhetoric, but in its original contribution to God's praise, the Book of Common Prayer (BCP), especially its 1662 variant. For, as the Church of England sought to heal divisions generated by its troubled birth, as well as the effects of a civil war a century later, and the theological divisions among Catholic and Protestant elements, the 1662 Prayer Book offered the Church and nation what they badly needed – a way to unite without the need to look too deeply into the souls and consciences of the people. It remains a founding gift of the Church.

However, another way of organising words – poetry – offers a key way of bringing out the distinctive joys of the Anglican inheritance. For, if it would be an act of folly to claim that Anglicanism is a uniquely poetic tradition, its poetry – which springs so often from a bold delight in the rhythms of the English found in the King James Bible, as well as the BCP – remains a joy.

Quantity is never a measure of quality, especially in an art form where fourteen lines can say much more than a thousand words of prose. Yet, for those who like things quantifiable, here's just a sample of the poets who might be claimed for Anglicanism: Donne, Herbert, Vaughan, Traherne, Eliot, Christina Rossetti, Auden, R. S. Thomas (in its Welsh variant), Geoffrey Hill and Rowan Williams to name a few. Oh, and Wordsworth and Betjeman. At the edges, one finds the likes of Wilfred Owen.

For some, reading that list might be troubling. They will want to distinguish between poets who – like Herbert – might be said to "make" pictures of Anglicanism's possibilities in their work and those – perhaps like Auden – for whom being Anglican offered a kind of thematic background. I'm happy for people to be troubled. Arguably, one of the joys of Anglicanism lies in its porous boundaries and wideness. To be Anglican is to be free of the need for doctrinaire safety or dogmatism; it is to find oneself somehow shaped by and attached to the wide Anglican way of going on, in worship, thought and prayer.

Poetry is a kind of alchemy. It makes wonder in the commonplace of language, using language (usually tired and worn) to achieve miracle. The Anglican "tradition" of poetry – if there be such a defined thing – is a miracle of invention. In the early seventeenth century, what was the Church of England's theology and polity to be? What, indeed, was "England", and "English" as a language? The most educated English poets could write in Latin or French or Italian. The alchemic joy of an emergent Anglican poetry lay in its making of a language vibrant not only with rhetorical force, but with music.

Donne's *Divine Meditations* – not marked by obvious joy, but by the thoughts of a poet working out his faith in the face of God's terrifying love – show poetry in movement with new possibilities in English. Most are Petrarchan in form, yet some show signs of Shakespeare's influence on the sonnet. If the Petrarchan sonnet is noted for its capacity for argument, the incorporation of Shakespearean elements perhaps signals a new trust in the possibilities of love. Donne writes, "Oh my black soul! now thou art summoned/By sickness, death's herald, and champion." The sonnet opens with startling honesty and is met by a volta of apparently easy conventionality: "Yet, grace, if thou repent, thou canst not lack". Donne's genius is to develop this in quite visceral, yet beautiful ways:

> Oh make thyself with holy mourning black,
> And red with blushing, as thou art with sin;
> Or wash thee in Christ's blood, which hath this might
> That being red, it dyes red souls to white.

There is delight, sensuality and joy in this tension and it indicates a path into metaphysical joy and wonder pursued by Traherne and Vaughan and, most especially, George Herbert.

Yet there is more. Donne's "Batter My Heart, Three-Personed God" is justly famous. It gestures to a profound analogue to joy – terror. It is striking because it is uncomfortable, indicating the violence that lurks close to the mystery of the Trinity; its familiarity with human conflict and the fragility of goodness. This is no image of a pale Galilean[1] or a domestic god. This is poetry as *eros*. Donne requires of God, "Take me to you, imprison me… /… ravish me." This is language at breaking point. When it reaches there it either collapses or, as in Donne's case, remakes itself anew.

There's a reason Herbert is held in such high esteem in Anglicanism and beyond: he achieves poetry which is almost impossibly clever, yet simple. His poems are like a concentrated version of the Church of England's settlement: paradoxical and yet liveable. Lines like "Love bade me welcome. Yet my soul drew back/Guilty of dust and sin" are justly famous. There are, of course, echoes of biblical rhythms (most notably the Song of Songs), but the technical achievement in the poem is startling, deploying iambic pentameter along with short lines. This is sensuous joy allied to linguistic mastery. The boldness of Herbert is indicated in the intimacy of address: "And know you not, says Love, who bore the blame?/My dear, then I will serve." He is biblical, he is modern and he remains fresh.

Several postmodern critics, including Antony Easthope and Julia Kristeva, have suggested that iambic pentameter is not to be taken as a neutral form, but as ideological. Easthope notes that it is especially suited for the voice of privilege, becoming the poetic metre of the Tudor courts, relegating older accentual forms to a secondary, "folk" status.[2] In English, pentameter became the dominant form for at least four centuries.

Insofar as there is truth in this (and I think there is) perhaps one of the question marks over the Anglican poetic tradition is the extent to which it is tied up in authority and privilege. Clearly, of all the Christian traditions in Britain, the Church of England is tied up with establishment and privilege. Yet, ironically, perhaps because Anglicanism has tended to be "discreet" on matters of doctrine or, in the very least, has encouraged a certain wideness in its interpretation, its poets have rarely felt called to be doctrinaire. There is little safety in Anglican poetry's imagination.

If the language of Anglicanism has been over-identified with privilege and position, there are grounds for asking, "Where are all the women poets?" This is, of course, a serial issue in all poetry. Until the "triumph" of the novel in the nineteenth century, poetry was the ultimate masculine art form. It was the province of Wordsworthian "artists" wanting to touch the Sublime or – later – Tennyson trying to reconstruct poetry's Round Table in epics like "Idylls of the King". In comparison, Cecil Frances Alexander

---

1 "Thou hast conquered, O pale Galilean; the world has grown grey from thy breath". From Algernon Charles Swinburne, "Hymn to Proserpine".

2 "Antony Easthope, *Poetry as Discourse* (London: Routledge, 1983).

(of "All Things Bright and Beautiful" fame) might offer adequate verse, but she offers questionable poetry.

Christina Rossetti is more than an exception. She is a reminder that the canon of poetry, Anglican or otherwise, can be reconstructed and remade. Her reputation has gone through various iterations in the past one hundred and fifty years. At the turn of the twentieth century, Rossetti was seen as a writer whose poetry revealed the invisible world of her faith. However, by the 1990s, she was read as a highly intelligent woman whose poetry negotiates victimisation, whilst being subversively feminist.

What is clear now is that her poetry – dazzlingly balanced between the influence of John Keble's theology of reserve and a delight in language – sits at the Victorian top table. Her devotional poetry – often dismissed by feminist and formalist critics alike as simpering and lacking the bravery of early work like "Goblin Market" – is increasingly appreciated for its suppleness and sensitivity. If much poetry can feel like dust in the mouth, Rossetti's poetry – grounded in her Anglo-Catholicism – sings. The riches of the fruit in "Goblin Market" ("Apples and quinces,/Lemons and oranges,/Plump unpeck'd cherries,/Melons and raspberries,/Bloom-down-cheek'd peaches") explode in the mouth, while the wider poem reworks the meaning of the Eucharist as grounded in love between sisters. The poem is revolutionary.

Yet this liveliness, mutuality and communion is also a feature of her directly religious poetry. Rossetti's second "St Peter" sonnet echoes Peter's denial. Rossetti requests the Divine to look her "eye to eye":

> Lord, I have heard the crowing of the cock
> And have not wept: ah, Lord, Thou knowest it.
> Yet still I hear Thee knocking, still I hear:
> "Open to Me, look on Me eye to eye,
> That I may wring thy heart and make it whole;
> And teach thee love because I hold thee dear,
> And sup with thee in gladness soul with soul,
> And sup with thee in glory by and by."
>
> (ll. 7-14)

This is sensuously immediate. God is imagined knocking persistently at the door of the poet's heart, something underlined by the repetition of the image of God knocking – in lines two ("Lord, dost Thou stand and knock") and nine. There is a suggestion in this poem of a recasting of Donne's "Batter My Heart, Three-Personed God", yet as Esther Hu reminds us, if Donne's sonnet is violent in its imagery, "Rossetti's sequence of verbs evokes calm courtesy."[3] This then is a picture of poet and Christ in relationship, engaged in mutual love. Both the poet (as one who prays) and Christ (as the God who hears) is permitted to speak and perform subjectivity. Theirs is a mutuality of love which requites the other.

Whatever else the Great War achieved (or destroyed) it made available new poetries. It is dangerous to make too much of the fact that Wilfred Owen once considered Anglican Holy Orders. However, the poet whom everyone knows brought a seared picture of faith into the trenches. Indeed, as Alan Wilkinson argues, "the majority of his war poems show him testing biblical and Christian images and doctrines to see whether they will bear the weight of the increasing revulsion he felt against the slaughter."[4]

In one of his letters, Owen suggests:

> Christ is literally in no man's land. There men often hear His voice: Greater love hath no man than this, that a man lay down his life – for a friend. Is it spoken in English only and French? I do not believe so. Thus you see how pure Christianity will not fit in with pure patriotism… Christians have deliberately cut some of the main teaching of their code.[5]

There is no more joy in Owen's poetry than there is in Roman Catholic war poets like David Jones or the post-war convert Sassoon, or a Jewish poet like Rosenberg. Owen said that his subject was war and the pity of war. The Anglicanism lies in the tension.

Perhaps, like all once ubiquitous figures, T. S. Eliot's reputation has gone through revision in recent decades. There is no doubt, however, that, along with Ezra Pound, he remade Anglophone poetry after the First World War. Modernism and its obsession with language may bewilder and annoy, but Eliot's Prufrock and the strange figures who march out from the pages of "The Waste Land" are icons of our fractured modern selves. For many people of faith, "Four Quartets" represents Eliot's abiding achievement – a balance between his erudition, experiments with language and a faith both mystic and intelligent. His poetry makes a case for his claim that "genuine poetry can communicate before it is understood".

If I am trying to suggest that the joy of Anglicanism's poetry lies as much in its tensions and balance between polarities, then for me it also lies in

---

3 Esther T. Hu, "Christina Rossetti, John Keble, and the Divine Gaze", in *Victorian Poetry*, 46:2 (2008), 175-189.
4 Alan Wilkinson, "The Church of England and the First World War" (London: SPCK, 1978), 113.
5 Harold Owen and John Bell (eds), *Wilfred Owen: Collected Letters* (London: Oxford University Press, 1967), 562.

its bold questioning of received doctrine. Anglicanism finds in at least some of its poets a testing out of the limits of orthodoxy. Auden offers a fascinating case in point. Upon his return to Anglicanism in the 1940s, he brought to bear an independent, non-dogmatic intelligence. He was, as he wrote in "Horae Canonicae: Terce", alert to the religious tendency to indulge in our own "secret cult". We do tend to pray to an image of ourselves. He was unafraid of unorthodoxy, even heresy, suggesting to friends that he believed in patripassianism, the belief that the Father suffered with the Son.

If Auden's poetic gifts negotiated by turns the varieties of passion – spiritual, sexual, and political – Geoffrey Hill's testing of the possibilities of faith and words are severe, erudite and startling. Hill went so far as to say that some of great poetry "recognises that words fail us". The poet and Hill critic Jeffrey Wainwright has claimed that "the first wonder of poetry lies in the immediate effects of language".[6] Hill's difficult language – alert to the rhythms of the seventeenth century as much as internet speak – wrestles the Anglican inheritance into the modern and postmodern age. He empties language of self and says that if we are to be people of faith we must be unafraid of the recalcitrance of language.

Unorthodoxy, even heresy, might be the privilege of the poet seeking new ways of wrangling language, but what of the priest-poet? R. S. Thomas has become, for many in the Anglican Churches and beyond, the go-to religious poet. For many Anglicans, he is the one "contemporary" poet they know. More importantly, he articulates a picture of faith recognisable to the educated worshipper in postmodern times – that God is found in absence rather than presence. His language presents one kind of response to Arnold's famous lines in "Dover Beach" – "The Sea of Faith/Was once, too, at the full, and round earth's shore/Lay like the folds of a bright girdle furled." In a poem like "The Empty Church", Thomas presents a picture of the church as a stone "lure" for God. Candles are offered as a temptation to bring forth a moth-like God who cannot resist the light. Time and again in his poetry, Thomas enters the space of faith only to discover God retreating as if into another room.

This is hardly comforting or comfortable faith. This is poetry wrought out of Thomas' tough context – the wild terrain of Wales where sun and light can be fleeting, where rain and storm are always close. In what sense is there joy to be found? Well, for sure, joy is not the same as pleasure. Thomas' poetry is not comfortable, pleasing or ravishing. However, it is

6 Jeffrey Wainwright, *Acceptable Words: Essays on the Poetry of Geoffrey Hill* (Manchester: University Press, 2005), 1.

real. The Jesuit writer Gerard Hughes suggested that "God is in the facts". Insofar as that is true, then God is to be found where we find ourselves. "Reality" – even one constructed through words – is the ground and wellspring of joy, even if that joy is structured through a life lived in wilderness, God's absence, and longing rather than fulfilment. Joy is seeing more of the truth of God.

The world, then, has perhaps become a difficult place for both faith and poetry. Joy is chastened, a matter of glimpses. Perhaps Anglicanism's traditions of finding a *via media* which brings together scripture, tradition and reason represents a way of meeting chastened joy. The poetry of Rowan Williams – grounded in the Eastern Orthodox mystic's sense of wonder as well as Hegelian rigour – offers an example of holy joy in a compromised world. For Williams, the poetic voice, even in the silence of waiting, has not been silenced. It searches for sense in dialectical encounter between world and word. Rowan Williams captures this rather beautifully in the poem "Emmaus" when talking of the "solid stranger" who "fills up" the pilgrims as they walk the road. We discover that we must "carry him with us". When he breaks bread, it begins to rain and our voices – freed by the Christ – "shine" with his living water. Our faithful, honest poet-priest Christ offers us nothing more or less than the truth. And it is not comfortable and rarely comforting.

I began this chapter with a quote from Christina Rossetti: "There's blood between us, love, my love." "The Convent Threshold" is a dramatic monologue, ripe with irony. The speaker might be addressing a lover as she is about to deny "self" by entering one of the (then new) Anglican sisterhoods; she might be speaking from beyond the grave. The poem negotiates a world caught between fallenness and redemption: "My lily feet are soiled with mud,/With scarlet mud which tells a tale/Of hope that was, of guilt that was,/Of love that shall not yet avail." The speaker claims, of her lover, that "Your eyes look earthward, mine look up."

It is true that all Christian traditions are caught between world and heaven, body and spirit and so on; the fact that our God knows incarnation means we have to be serious about the meaning of joy and glory in this life, as much as in heaven. However, the Anglican inheritance in poetry offers the most extraordinary riches when considering the question of what it means to share in God's joy and delight in creation. Anglican poetry has proven unafraid of the terrors of a language that cannot be controlled. It richly delights in complexity and compromise and has found in the "blood" and body of this life the words to speak heaven.

Perhaps that all sounds too grand and rhetorical. Even when it does, it is towards the poetry that I'm drawn. When I am tired, or lost, or wrestling with doubt and fear because of a tragedy in the world, or just a horrid, tiring day, I find that Donne or Herbert or Hill can take the weight and strain. Like good liturgy, I find the power of Anglican poetry lies in the fact that it can be tested by my and the world's troubles and not be found wanting. That, perhaps, is its final value, justification and joy.

The Joy of the Family for an Anglican

by Ruth Gledhill

Ruth is editor of *Christian Today* magazine. Prior to that she was Religion Correspondent for *The Times*. She is the daughter of a vicar and, as a result of her father's calling, grew up in Jamaica, Barbados and various parts of England and Wales. For all its faults, Ruth loves being an Anglican. Given all her own many faults, she considers herself extremely blessed now to be part of a large, extended and very modern family. She is married to Alan Franks, a writer and musician, and they have one teenage son. Alan also has three children and four grandchildren from his first marriage. Ruth plays the clarinet for the London Gallery Quire which sings a repertoire of West Gallery Music from the time of Thomas Hardy and beyond. The quire rehearses in one of her favourite churches in all the world, St James Garlickhythe in the City of London.

In my professional past I have been, if not an anachronism, then something of a minority in Fleet Street newsrooms. For more than twenty-five years I belonged to the vanishing breed of full-time religion correspondents, and there were indeed occasions when I did experience a sense of isolation akin to that which must be felt by an endangered species. It wasn't exactly that God had been somehow disinvented by the owners and editors of national papers, but that he (or should that be she?) had fallen into a state of – forgive the word – unnewsworthiness – a figure to be wheeled out and decorated with all the conventional clichés of Fleet Street on the big days of the religious calendar.

I knew, and had always known, that there was more to the institutions of Anglican faith than this. Indeed, I had been reared in a series of vicarages and seminaries and, in a way that has remained vital to my life, in a number of ways had downloaded the rhythms of the ecclesiastical year into the centre of my being – my soul, indeed.

Sure, the life of a vicar's daughter did entail moving around – from draughty, under-heated, decrepit but beautiful rectories to new-build red brick boxes on estates. True, this life sometimes verged on the peripatetic and insecure. And yet the presence of Anglicanism in my life did, and still does, provide me with a sense of stability that is as welcome as it is sometimes surprising.

Growing up in the Church gave me an extended family that you don't necessarily have to be a vicar's daughter to have and enjoy – especially in the way that the modern Church operates with home groups, Bible groups, Lent groups, reading groups – the list is endless. I suppose we were very much a family of the Church. In the years since then I have found myself wondering to what extent the Church itself can be considered as another form of family. In our particular family there were sometimes truly blurred lines between the Church and our family unit.

At one point our father was in charge of a tiny Georgian gem of a church in Gratwich, Staffordshire, with a congregation of about sixty souls. Many Sundays, the only people in church would be our mother, we five siblings, the churchwarden and the organist. There were also the organist's daughters, whose beautiful voices deserved a far wider audience. Perhaps it was not surprising that for years, when our father said: "Praise be to God," one of our sisters interpreted this as "Praise Peter God." His name was Peter, and she thought he was, literally, God.

But let me for a moment banish the mists of nostalgia and record this childhood in as clear-eyed way as I can. Our mother was about as far as it is possible to get from the cosy and conventional archetype of a vicar's wife in rural post-war England. She was busy all right – who wouldn't be with five children born in eleven years, foster children in substantial numbers and horses, dogs, cats and rabbits that seemed to multiply at a biblical rate? Not that they lacked their uses. One pony even provided our transport to school. We had an old rag-and-bone cart, and the teasing was merciless, earning us the nickname "The Waltons".

Sometimes we lived in incredible poverty. At one point, the Church rescued us from a time when my father had tried secular work as a teacher. That ended unhappily and for a time he was on the dole. Being blessed by moving to a beautiful location and living in a Queen Anne rectory was better than that experience, but still the financial reality was bleak beyond words. I don't suppose I will ever forget the sight of my mother peeling up the cheap synthetic swirly multicoloured 1970s carpets to take them into this rectory. The walls and ceilings were covered by paintings of beautiful flowers, done by the previous vicar's wife. We found out she had done this to paint over the cracks when the ceiling plaster began to tumble down over our heads. She had also painted little roses and eaves around the mouse holes in the kitchen.

Our mother, who solved the mouse problem by simply importing a few hungry cats, really did her best on the stipend, shopping at the local bulk-buy outlet, but I remember what it was like to be extremely hungry. We were also among many families who suffered through the apparently interminable strikes of the 1970s, doing O level revision by candlelight. So she was the wife of a vicar and a good wife of a good vicar – but a vicar's wife, putting on smart dinners for the local worthies and the bishop as vicars were expected to do in those days – no. Her hands were simply far too full of children, animals and simply trying to find enough for us to eat to lay on anything remotely approaching a parish tea.

Then there was our father (or should that be Our Father?) He was a delightful, kind, formidable and eccentric man. He had been a classics scholar at Balliol College in Oxford and remained to the end of his life a man of broad and questing intellect. What impresses me all the more as I get older is the way in which he turned out his sermons so diligently, Sunday after Sunday, to congregations regularly made up of little more than his own family.

Through all this, the Church was of immense succour and support to us and our neighbours. Although confidentiality always ruled, in our small community we did pick up on the troubles that were suffered by many who were worse off than we were – those with unstable families, or going through the penal system, or the farmers who were depressed and sometimes completely defeated by the growing mountains of bureaucracy and mechanisation that seemed to be turning their lives and livelihoods upside down.

And our father took the Church's mission seriously in helping these people – talking to them, visiting them, being a completely trustworthy resource who they trusted all the more for knowing of his own difficulties. They knew that he was coping with poverty, with difficult children (stroppy me in particular), and with the contrast between his Rugby-Oxford education and the reality of life in a rural Staffordshire parish where little had changed since the 1950s, but which was just beginning to feel the tremors of the fast pace of transformation that has since sent shockwaves through so many areas of life.

At the heart of life in a country parish, and in the suburban parish church that I attend today, is the Church's traditional role of "hatching, matching and dispatching", being an enduring presence from the start to the end of life. The Church has gone wrong in so many ways. But where it has gone right is in its ability to understand and nurture family. Although the two phenomena cannot necessarily be empirically linked, declining churchgoing has coincided with an increase in family breakdown. We read a lot about the Church failing to connect with the young. But where the Church has managed to make it work – I'm thinking of an evangelical church I attend sometimes near our home – the sense of positive connection with teenagers and young adults and the joy of children being born, baptised, then moving through the different Sunday and evening groups that cater for them as they grow up is tangible.

Like so many in the Church, and some would say like the original Holy Family, my own circumstances have not met the Christian ideal. I'm married to someone who is not a believer. The Church should be a place where broken families can find healing. Writing as someone with a pretty broken past, I've found an immense variety of responses to brokenness in the modern Church. Anyone who has spent most of a long life trying to be regular at church – and admittedly having time away from it – will have experienced a variety of responses to brokenness in their own lives.

However well-meaning the lay or clergy person is when attempting to impart Christian advice to a person struggling with relationships and breakdown, resorting to unforgiving fundamentals should not still happen, although unfortunately it does.

On the other hand, the sacrament of reconciliation, when done well by a priest who truly understands and believes, is a thing of miracles still. For someone like me, who has been married more than once, there would have been a time, fortunately before my own, when I would have received a lot of criticism. At best, I might have been silently tolerated, even grudgingly forgiven. But at worst I could have been openly vilified and held up as a cautionary tale of how not to go about life. Unfortunately there are groups of people who still experience this kind of treatment.

Fortunately for people like me, the Church has found itself compelled to rethink some of its old moral absolutes. In this respect it is not all that dissimilar to other organisations. Yet some of these absolutes, it seems, must be hung onto at any cost – any cost at all. I find no contradiction in being married to someone who describes himself as agnostic. My husband has leanings and resources which I would describe as spiritual. When I do precisely that – i.e. describe his position on this or that as spiritual – he demurs. What he accepts, and more so by the day, is that there is a power of infinitely more greatness than ourselves. But he chooses not to define it. That is, he chooses not to because he feels himself unequal to the task and is happy not to make a fool of himself in the trying. One of his strongest convictions comes from Thomas Huxley, who is credited with the coinage of the word "agnostic" – meaning, quite literally, "without knowledge".

My husband is also one of those who believes that this word – agnostic – may well have been intended as a rebuke or at least a comic reference to the gnostics, thereby setting the logical position of uncertainty against the presumptuous one of utter sureness. He has many convictions, of which one of the strongest and most consistent is that he does not know. It is not that he wants to opt out of difficult moral debates – in fact he pursues them with admirable confessional integrity. A stated certainty about the existence of a God, let alone an omniscient God, and an incarnate son who rose from the dead, seems to him to be preposterous and even an abuse of mankind's own rationale, God-given though it is said to be. He tolerates my belief but sees it differently. Tolerance of other opinions, including a more literalist faith, is for him one of the primary ways of addressing disagreements between members of the human race. What appals him is the way in which unproven deities are invoked by members of so many religions in order to rubberstamp acts which are often venal and rapacious. In this his disapproval is little lower than that of the late self-described "antitheist", the polemicist Christopher Hitchens.

Having said all that, my husband gets enormous delight from singing in a West Gallery Quire – this being the music played in the country churches of England until the late nineteenth century and famously rhapsodised by the novels of Thomas Hardy, himself a notable fiddler, in *Under the Greenwood Tree*. Does he not see some contradiction, even running to hypocrisy, of a declared agnostic mouthing sentiments scripted by and for the devout? No, he is unrepentant, saying that just as you do not have to be in love to be moved by the spectacle of that force, so you do not require faith in order to be profoundly moved by those numinous feelings stirred by music in the human soul.

I mention this at a little length because it is an example of how a family can model life in the wider world. Although I am now editor of *Christian Today*, most of my working life has been in a strongly secular environment. Most churchgoers today will spend large parts of their lives among people who do not believe what they do, and who might even find something strange or odd about the beliefs of a Christian. This is just one of the ways that faith, practised at home as well as in the hour of the Sunday church service, can help us find a way to live and work in the wider world.

This is particularly the case with family, at the heart of its mission through its role in baptisms, marriages and funerals. This means that a person does not need a formal or declared faith in order to appreciate the fact that the Church, for all its shortcomings, is basically a good thing. As with the premature obituary of Mark Twain, reports of its demise are greatly exaggerated. True, church attendance may be in decline, but it still retains a quietly vital, even vibrant role in many areas of public and private life – not least among them, the family.

The features of the Anglican Communion being part of the establishment – bishops in the House of Lords, the Queen as Supreme Governor – are a contributory factor to there being respect for the position and teachings of the Church. I do not think that it is all bad that we still have these twenty-six anachronisms of the Lords Spiritual. It means that whether we are believers or not, there is still a place in the constitution for voices which address social and spiritual interests, rather than just the stridently political.

As moribund as both the Lords and the Church may sometimes appear to doubters, the fact remains that many of the most reasoned and enlightened arguments put forward in the Lords come from men and women on the bench of bishops. Like so many of us in our personal lives, myself included, the Church has made some terrible wrong turns. One of these has been the way in which it has responded to the issue of gender equality. From my seat at the ringside, where I had already been ensconced for several years when women priests were voted through, it took a shockingly long time for the Church to accept the need for women bishops. And now there is of course the question of homosexuality. This stems from the conservative, sometimes referred to as "orthodox", Christian belief in the nature of family, or specifically marriage – that it should be between a man and woman – based on texts in the Bible. The controversy is like a wound that won't heal. Many Christians, even evangelicals, do not take this view and believe the relevant Bible passages were born of a particular social context that no longer pertains. However, it is the conservative position that has held sway in the Church, enabling it to argue a particular exemption in law and making it explicitly illegal for Church of England churches to carry out same-sex marriage ceremonies.

It would take much more than the Church changing its mind for this situation to change. An actual change in the law would be needed before the Church of England could legally allow same-sex marriage. It remains a subject which draws such venomous attacks that it becomes hard to reconcile Christian orthodoxy with tolerance for other people's lives. It is ironic that, while the Catholic Church actually takes a similar conservative position to the Church of England, it is Pope Francis who has summed up the position for many Christians with his statement on the issue – "Who am I to judge?"

There is a terrible irony in this, with the Church apparently sabotaging its own recruitment drive by rejecting the life choices of a significant minority. Many church leaders have not understood that a lot of clergy think differently, or that the hurt felt by many LGBT people, who are also part of the Church family, is also deeply felt by their friends, families and the wider community. We are driving away many young adults who have grown up being taught that inclusion and diversity are good things.

Fortunately, however damaging this debate – and it risks being extremely so – there are a lot of positives. To this day the Church remains a force for immense social influence. With services under such strain, the Church is effectively one of the few remaining agencies whose members continue the profound Christian tradition of giving unconditional help to the needy.

Of course it was originally the Church – all the Churches – that were responsible for much healthcare, education and the welfare of orphans and the poor. This social and caring work of the Church was a long time ago and to a large degree taken over by the state, although of course the Churches still educate many children.

We are now in a time when the NHS, pioneered by the great Welsh socialist Nye Bevan in the 1940s and so successful in its provision for the sick and elderly until now, is itself well past three score and ten years and stretched to breaking point and beyond. Families on the breadline struggle to cope on available benefits – and this even includes those where people are working but find themselves unable to earn enough. Even now, in this supposedly secular age, in many towns, cities and rural areas, we find the Church filling the gaps in welfare provision, demonstrating the way in which it values families and their needs. Many food banks are run out of church premises, manned by volunteers from those churches.

Whether we like it or not, the noble dream of a welfare state which could subsume the supportive roles taken historically by the extended family is now characterised by shortfall and funding crises. And quietly, in an understated, modest, anonymous way, it is often local churches who are stepping in to plug the gaps. These days churches are often happy to work alongside other organisations in these endeavours, and it is now commonplace for churches to make their halls and rooms available for meetings of the twelve-step programmes that tackle addiction problems ranging from drink and drugs to depression and gambling. These twelve-step programmes, which began with Alcoholics Anonymous, are striking examples of the way in which Christian principles have been taken up and used to dramatic effect in the recovery movement by groups and individuals who may not necessarily have started out from a position of faith.

Separately from this, I have witnessed many clergy in inner-city areas at the forefront of working with young and older people struggling with poverty, addiction, depression and other social problems. The phenomenal Street Pastors movement, with its "flipflops and lollipops" approach, takes caring onto the streets in a non-proselytising, pastoral manner that is having remarkable effects in calming town centres throughout the country on Friday and Saturday nights.

If the Church is indeed a family, it is so both for better and for worse. It has authority figures who think they know best, and sometimes go on a bit too much; it has immense closeness in terms of empathy and sympathy, as well as rebellion against the centre, with young or new Christians struggling to make sense of it all.

During my years at *The Times*, witnessing decades of debate in the Church of England about secular and spiritual issues, I've been privileged to encounter some extraordinary people. In my own family, I've witnessed amazing courage and fortitude in the face of sometimes barely imaginable difficulty. And in becoming part of the life of our local church, I've been in awe at the quiet but effective service given to the community and to God.

I sometimes find myself looking at such people and wondering about the extent to which their apparent composure in the face of a discordant and sometimes chaotic world has been informed by faith. Or is it just that they are naturally that way? And while I can feel so much "less than" compared to these stalwarts, in my own liberal and inclusive traditional Anglican parish, I never feel judged. This daily application of unconditional love to the world is the kind I try to learn from, and apply to my own behaviour, in family, in church, in service to the community and in work.

None of us will find that our church or our families are perfect. But they are hard won, the best we've got. And they're not going under without a fight.

The Joy of Scripture for an Anglican

by the Revd Canon Dr Trevor Dennis

Trevor is an Anglican priest who has long been passionate about opening up the world of biblical scholarship to a wider audience. He retired in 2010 from his post as Vice Dean at Chester Cathedral, where he also had an education brief. Before Chester he taught Old Testament studies for nearly twelve years at Salisbury and Wells Theological College (now Sarum College), and it was there he started writing books. He now has fourteen to his name, plus a fifteenth, *The Circle of Peace: An Antidote to Distress*, which he wrote with a psychologist friend, Ken Lewis (SPCK, 2015). His other recent titles are, *God in Our Midst: Gospel Stories and Reflections* (SPCK, 2012), and *The Gospel beyond the Gospels* (SPCK, 2017). He is married to Caroline and they have four children and eight grandchildren.

The *joy* of scripture? Really? For an *Anglican*? Are you quite sure? I've always been an Anglican, so I should know. I was brought up to revere the Bible, to believe it and obey it, but no one ever spoke of me en*joy*ing it.

Oh, but I do! In the early 1980s I joined the staff of a theological college in Salisbury to teach Old Testament studies, and it was there that I gained a profound joy from grappling with biblical texts, and from entering into them more deeply than I had ever done before.

At the time academic *literary* studies of the Bible were in full swing, and I learned a simple but far-reaching lesson: in exploring biblical texts I was dealing with great art, with creative storytelling and poetry of the highest order.

I discovered why a work as miserable as Ecclesiastes, with its insistence that all is vanity and its thoroughly depressing view of old age at the end, was included by the Jews among their most treasured possessions and so given a place in that exclusive collection of writings we Christians call the Old Testament. It was because, as I discovered when I started to read the book in the Hebrew, it is written in the most exquisite lyric poetry. (And no doubt it was valued so highly because it captures aspects of human life and experience that are universal, and gives them powerful expression; it rings true and always will.)

Together with the students I found, again through the Hebrew, the stunning beauty of the opening chapters of Genesis, and its dream of a world where everything is in harmony, where there is no killing for food (for all animals, including human beings, are given plants to eat), where there is order, rhythm, blessing, fruitfulness and rest (even God rests in Genesis 2); a world which God can survey and declare, without hesitation or reservation, "Very good!"

Our research into the historical background of the poem (strictly speaking the Hebrew is mostly written in rhythmic prose, but it is best to think of it as poetry) revealed the startling significance of those famous verses about human beings made "in the image of God". For they were probably first composed at the time of the exile in Babylon, and after the Babylonian army had smashed Jerusalem and its temple to bits and ravaged both the towns and countryside of Judah and its people. Like other rulers in the ancient Near East, the king of Babylon proclaimed himself the image of a god. The language of being made in the image and likeness of God thus belonged to the palace at Babylon, in the corridors of its ruthless emperor.

And the unnamed Jewish poet of Genesis 1 sneaked into that palace one night and returned to the tents of his defeated people with the king's claims hidden in his pocket. Then he did something quite extraordinary with them. He didn't say to his people, "It's *our* king who is made in the image of God, not theirs!" He didn't say, "We, the Jews, are the ones made in the image of God, not the king of Babylon." Slipping into pure poetry, he said that *all human beings*, both men and women, are made in the image and likeness of God; *all human beings*, by their very creation, have royal status. In the circumstances he was being extremely generous, for "all human beings" included Babylonians. His words also represented one of the most radical and challenging political statements ever made, and they still do.

The students and I dug out the story of the Garden of Eden from beneath the rubble of the doctrines of the fall and original sin, and the toxic waste of centuries of careless misogyny. We found a sparkling, poignant tale of two children (why should we insist that Adam and Eve were created as adults?) who lived in a garden where they could hear God's footsteps and talk with God as natural as could be, but who were deceived by a talking snake which was cleverer than they were (this is a children's story in more ways than one), and who grew up too fast and came to know too much about the harsh realities of adult life awaiting them. We found much sadness there, for its ending tells of a breakdown of relationships between men and women, between human beings and the animal and plant worlds, and a tragic loss of intimacy between human beings and God – we can't hear God's footsteps any more.

We teased out the strands of the story of Shiphrah and Puah, the midwives of Exodus 1, who risked their lives by disobeying a cruel pharaoh's orders to kill at birth any boy babies born to the Hebrew women being held in the slave camps. It is a terrifying tale, and one of its most knee-wobbling moments is when the pharaoh summons Shiphrah and Puah to his palace a second time. He knows full well they haven't killed a single baby. Surely, we think, they won't get out of this one alive. The last thing we expect is a joke. It's hidden in the Hebrew and we needed the writings of Jonathan Magonet, a Jewish scholar, to reveal it to us.

"Well, you see, Your Royal Ever-So-Divine Highness," the midwives say (in a manner of speaking – my version), "it's like this. Those Hebrew women, they're just like animals – they have their babies so quick. They just drop 'em, and by the time we arrive the husband comes out and says, 'You're too late. She's had it already.'"

It's all a lie, of course, but their explanation appeals to the pharaoh's racism (those Hebrew women; quite unlike your refined Egyptian ladies!), and to his misogyny (they're animals, not human beings). And it works! He believes them and lets them go, and were it not for his command to his own people to throw the Hebrew babies into the Nile, the story would be a triumph in every sense. Shiphrah and Puah are among the bravest and cleverest characters in the Bible, and among the most faithful, too, for they act not only out of love for the mothers and their babies, but out of their devotion to God. Rarely have they been given their due. The students and I, with the help of Jonathan Magonet,[1] did our best to put that right.

Sometimes in our studies our jaws dropped at the daring of the passages we were studying, when all caution seemed to have been thrown to the winds. Take the example of Genesis 32, where Jacob wrestles through the dark hours of the night with God. Christian preachers, never mind Anglican ones, have generally talked of him wrestling with an angel. Yet if you look carefully at the passage, you will see it is God who is there. Remember, this is creative storytelling of the most profound and adventurous kind. We Anglicans have often been taught to play it safe. There's no striving for safety here! And the story has a greater surprise still. In the course of the wrestling match Jacob seems for a time to have God at his mercy. "Let me go!" God cries. Surely this is too far removed from the careful world of Anglican doctrine! But what happens if we take Jacob's story to Golgotha, and read it out at the foot of the cross? We look into the eyes of the man hanging there, and we see, to our horror, a God at our mercy – only this time we are out to destroy that God.

The story of Jesus' death is the Bible's most daring story of all. We Christians, as Paul reminded the new Church in Corinth, have a highly problematic tale to tell about God. It concerns the crucifixion by the Romans of a pesky, controversial rabbi from an obscure village in Galilee. Pilate sentences him to the most brutal, degrading, excruciating death in the Roman repertoire – death by slow suffocation on a cross. All four Gospels have this death as their climax. They build up to it inexorably, turning, turning the screw with deft strokes of their pen. Once at Golgotha, they linger for a while. Though Matthew gets carried away with talk of an earthquake and bodies coming out of their tombs, they generally use much restraint in their telling, except when it comes to the significance they place on the event. It is, so they all say – John most clearly – the great Moment of Truth, when God is revealed, when the curtain across the Holy of Holies is

---

1 Jonathan Magonet, *Bible Lives* (London: SCM, 1992), 7.

torn down, and God steps into the open. Peter, James and John may have had their Transfiguration scene already (at least in Mark, Matthew and Luke), but this, the death of Jesus, represents a Transfiguration scene for all humankind, for all eternity. Its thick darkness, which seems to undo the very creation itself and return it to the wild and waste of Genesis 1:2, is ablaze with the love of God! It is a paradox to beat all paradoxes.

The women disciples discover the truth of it all first, not at Golgotha itself, though they are there looking on, but when they go to Jesus' tomb and find it buzzing not with flies but with angels; when they are met by the risen Jesus now clothed in the technicolour dreamcoat that God wore at creation; in the case of Mary of Magdala, when she hears him say her name (what a moment that is! Surely one of the greatest in the entire corpus of biblical literature – and one I find peculiarly difficult to get right when I read it aloud).

The crucifixion story might be the boldest tale of all, but there are others that exhibit a similar un-Anglican lack of caution. In John 13, at the last meal they will share together before his death, Jesus washes the feet of his friends. If we are not careful, we will be too familiar with this story and with the piety laid upon it to be surprised by it, let alone shocked. But Peter is shocked all right, so John tells us. No wonder. Most people washed their own feet when they crossed a threshold of a house, including their own, and especially before meals. The very rich would have a slave to do it for them. But it was thought such a demeaning task that it would be given to the young slave girls right at the bottom of the domestic pile. And here is Jesus, with a towel round his waist, kneeling at his friends' feet, washing them as best he can, and drying them with the towel! "I am among you as one who serves," Jesus says in Luke 22:27. Here in John his actions speak louder than words. Indeed only one thing he does in the Gospels speaks more clearly of who he is than this, and that is when he spreads his arms on the cross, trying to embrace his violent world. Jesus shows us God. Thus we learn from John 13 that God does not sit on a high throne for our fear, but kneels to wash our feet. It is mind-blowing, soul-blowing. I was not brought up to look *down* to find God! I was encouraged all the time to look up to him as the King of kings. (In all the Gospels, in fact, Jesus never behaves like a king – rabbi, prophet, teacher, healer, storyteller, poet, all these, but never a king.)

Even that is not the end of it, however, for in John 12, just one chapter earlier, Mary of Bethany kneels to anoint Jesus' feet and dry them with her hair. Her sister Martha has told him that he is the Messiah, the Son of

God (John 11:27). Mary shows him that if indeed he is to be the Messiah, the Son of God, the Word who was in the beginning with God, the Word who is God, then he must wash feet. John presents Mary of Bethany as Jesus' teacher. He embraces the status of a slave and, taught by one of his closest and dearest disciples, performs a slave's most demeaning task.

What joy is here! What profound challenge for our own living and that of our Christian communities!

"But wait a minute!" I hear you say. "You've been picking out all the best bits. What about the rest?!" Well, not *all* the best bits, by any stretch of the imagination. I could go on and on, for page upon page, 'til there was no room for any other contributor in this book. But you have a point: there *are* passages in the Bible, in both Testaments, which, if we are honest, are deeply troubling, and some, if we are completely honest, that are appalling. In my experience this is something Anglicans are very shy of saying, at least outside the high walls of academia. In all my years I have never heard a single sermon, at least beyond the confines of the theological college chapel in Salisbury, and beyond those I have preached myself, when the preacher has taken the Bible to task and said, "This simply won't do." "Difficult" passages are ignored altogether, or their difficulties smoothed over. "The Bible is always right" seems to be the consistent message, in both liberal and more conservative churches.

The Bible is not always right. For a start, women are largely written out of it, in both Testaments. Exodus may begin with Shiphrah and Puah, and tell us of the compassion and bravery of the pharaoh's daughter and her slave women, but the stories of these women are designed to bring Moses on stage, and from then on he, with God, dominates proceedings right up to the end of Deuteronomy. In the case of the Gospels, despite the wonderful stories of Mary and Martha and Mary of Magdala, we have to look very hard indeed before we realise that Jesus' closest disciples were probably women (the hints are there!). And when Luke's narrative moves from his Gospel into the book of Acts, we lose sight of those women completely, with one last tantalising glimpse of them given in Acts 1:14.

And sometimes, let's face it, the Bible is very wrong. Two examples will have to suffice: the story of the capture of Jericho in Joshua 6, and the parable of the unforgiving slave in Matthew 18.

Around the turn of the millennium I used a sabbatical to write a version of the Bible for children and young people (it's for adults as well, really, but don't tell anyone) called *The Book of Books*. How was I going to deal with the Jericho story? I knew my editor would want me to cover it; it's too well known. It tells of the annihilation of an entire population – it spells it out: men, women, children, domestic animals. Why are they massacred? Because they are in the wrong place at the wrong time; because the people of God have crossed the Jordan and are taking possession of their promised land, and Jericho is in the way. This would remain but a story of the terrible brutalities of war and conquest, if it weren't for the part that God plays in it. The storyteller goes out of his or her way to tell us the slaughter is planned by God, enabled by God and approved of by God. It turns God into a ruthless army commander, without any feeling or mercy towards those regarded as enemies. In my own version I refused to stop at the point where the walls fall flat and avoid any mention of the carnage. That would have been dishonest. All I could do was change the vantage point, so we were inside Jericho looking out, have a fearful silence settle over the place after the slaughter, and finally include a reminder of the command to Abraham and his descendants (the Hebrew of Genesis 12:2 presents it as a command, though it doesn't look like it in most translations) to be a blessing to all the families of the earth.

But with the parable in Matthew 18 I could do nothing. I had to leave it out altogether. For me, it is an ugly tale, with no shred of true beauty in it, and its conclusion is disastrous. The king in the parable condemns the unforgiving slave to be tortured until he has paid all he owes him. The debts are enormous. He will never be able to repay. So the king is effectively sentencing him to be tortured slowly, relentlessly to death. And then Matthew has Jesus say, "So my heavenly Father will also do to every one of you, if you do not forgive your brother or sister from your heart" (Matthew 18:35). That turns God into a torturer and a monster. And God is not a monster. God's goodness, compassion and love exceed anything we can imagine, far beyond those of the best, the most loving and compassionate of human beings. Otherwise God would not be God. I do not believe for one moment that Jesus said those words that Matthew puts into his mouth. There may well be a genuine parable of Jesus deep buried in the passage, but as it stands it must come from Matthew himself and his own persecuted Christian community. It is too much at odds with the Jesus we see and hear elsewhere in the Gospels, including Matthew. Is it not in Matthew, after all, that we hear Jesus say, "You have heard that it was said, 'You shall love your neighbour and hate your enemy.' But I say to you, love your enemies, and pray for those who persecute you"? (Matthew 5:43-44). Here is an authentic voice! *This* makes God audible!

I can hear you interrupting me again. "Hold on a minute! I thought this was supposed to be about the *joy* of scripture. Where's the joy in passages like that?" Where indeed? But we cannot touch the joy to be found in the Bible and cherish it unless we are honest about the darkness that resides in some of its pages. Otherwise we cannot teach or preach with integrity. People will see through us, and then we risk turning them away from the Bible altogether. If they do that, they will miss the countless treasures it has to offer.

Yet I concede that Joshua 6 and Matthew 18 do not give us the note on which to end. Jonah will make for a much better conclusion!

When I taught at Salisbury, I used to introduce many of the ordinands to the Old Testament through the story of Jonah. After exploring the text with them, I would ask them to prepare a dramatisation. We would clear the room so they had plenty of space, and… ("Oh no! He's going to say they had a whale of a time!") yes, we had a whale of a time. But not just with the scene of the big fish and Jonah praying to God from its belly in words so impossibly self-centred (again more obvious in the Hebrew) that they make the fish vomit. There is plenty of hilarity to be had before the fish swims into sight and plenty more after it has disappeared. The story of Jonah has a pantomime prophet, a pantomime ship's crew, a pantomime storm as well as a pantomime fish, a pantomime king in Nineveh with his pantomime people and their pantomime animals; and near the end God supplies a pantomime plant to give the despairing Jonah some shade from the pantomime sun. Even God in this tale is a pantomime figure… until the end, when, stepping out of costume, God asks, "Should I not care about Nineveh?" Suddenly the humour that has filled the whole story evaporates. The question is a very serious one indeed, especially when we recall that Nineveh was once the capital of Assyria, the city of a king and a people who had wreaked terrible havoc in Israel. The devastation was probably long past when Jonah came to be written, but Nineveh had lived on in the minds of the Jews as a symbol of ruthless oppression, just as Berlin and Auschwitz will be remembered among Jews for centuries to come. "Should I not care about Nineveh?" It is one of the great questions of the Bible, as important now as it was then. The storyteller leaves it hanging in the air. Quite deliberately he doesn't tell us how Jonah responds. In the silence that follows we find that *we* have to answer it, substituting for Nineveh whatever might be our own centre of oppression.

And there, for this Anglican at least, is the real joy (and the mighty challenge) of scripture!

The Joy of Vocation
for an Anglican

by the Very Revd John Witcombe

John is Dean of Coventry, responsible for Coventry Cathedral, with its international ministry of reconciliation. Having initially studied law, he has been ordained for over thirty years and has worked in both ministry and training in the Church in a wide variety of social and geographical contexts throughout England. For seven years before his current role he was Director of Ordinands, and then Director of Discipleship and Ministry in the Diocese of Gloucester. He now leads a large and varied team of paid staff and volunteers, each playing their part in the life and work of the cathedral. He is married to Ricarda, a hospital chaplain in Nuneaton.

Almighty and everlasting God,
by whose Spirit the whole body of the Church
     is governed and sanctified:
hear our prayer which we offer for all your
     faithful people,
that in their vocation and ministry
they may serve you in holiness and truth
to the glory of your name;
through our Lord and Saviour Jesus Christ,
who is alive and reigns with you,
in the unity of the Holy Spirit,
one God, now and for ever.[1]

Vocation – for everyone – is at the heart of Anglican identity. Everyone has a part to play, and that part is recognised and blessed by the Church in a kaleidoscope of moving patterns and colours that enrich one another and allow light to shine through the whole Church and into the world.

With its roots in both Catholic and Reformed tradition, there are key roles both for priests and lay people in Anglicanism. There is an order to the Church, which is entrusted to those who are ordained to a representative ministry of oversight and service. However, each member is free and expected to respond personally and obediently to God in their own way, as a part of the whole. It is common to hear people speak in rather mystical tones of a person "having a vocation" or "hearing a call", as though this were something peculiar to those entering ordained ministry. But this would miss something fundamentally important in our common life – that everyone has a vocation.

Vocation, discipleship and ministry – baptism and confirmation

The word "vocation" comes from the Latin word for "calling". The Christian life begins, as it did for those who first met Jesus by the Sea of Galilee, when we respond to the call of Jesus to follow. Faith leads to following, and following leads to coming to know Jesus and being sent by him into ministry. So vocation is neither a standalone thing nor a possession – it is not something you "have", like a certificate on the shelf. It is born out of relationships – with Jesus, and also with the Church. And it needs to be lived out as an expression of those relationships.

1 *Common Worship*, Collect for Ministry. www.churchofengland.org/prayer-worship/worship/texts/collects-and-post-communions/contemporary-language/specialoccasions.aspx, accessed 25 May 2017.

Jesus does not just call individuals to serve him simply as individuals, but he invites us to join a community of people following him. When I began to think, at the age of twenty, that I might have a vocation to ordained ministry, I was already living out my Christian life in relationship with my local church and community of Christians, and finding ways to play my part.

BAPTISM

So the first vocation that all Christians share is the vocation to follow Jesus, as disciples, within the life of the Church. For many Anglicans, our first response to that most fundamental calling started with our baptism as infants. It may seem strange that a response might be made before we can decide for ourselves – but that simply reinforces the fundamental corporate character of vocation for Anglicans. We may only discover what decision or response has been made on our behalf later in life, but that does not take away from the fact that (as part of our Christian family) we have been responding to the call of Jesus, as part of the Church, since our baptism.

The questions asked at baptism are questions of vocation: "Do you turn to Christ?" If we are wondering where our vocation lies, it's worth going right back to basics and allowing ourselves to hear those questions again, as if for the first time.

This is how the Church in Wales website puts it:

> All of us have particular talents and abilities. We do them because we enjoy them. But more importantly because they give us a sense of fulfilment and help us to serve God.

> A vocation is something that we believe God calls us to do. Every single one of us has a calling, a vocation, and we all need to try to work out what it is.

> What is God calling you to?

> There are many opportunities in the Church for you to use your talents and abilities to serve God's community.[2]

The Church of England's vocations pages remind us of our vocation in the world, coming out of our baptism:

> Our first calling is to live life in all its fullness and to represent Christ in the world.

---

2 www.churchinwales.org.uk/work-with-us/explore-your-vocation, accessed 4 June 2017.

This is our common calling as Christians.

> All who are baptised are called to ministry, whether that is lay or ordained. The Church needs a wide variety of ministers in order to serve all people. God calls young people and older ones, wealthy and poorer. The Church's ministers come from all walks of life, social classes, ethnic backgrounds and educational abilities.[3]

The introduction to the baptism service affirms both the *calling* and the *corporate* character of that primary, fundamental vocation to follow Christ:

> Faith is the gift of God to his people.
> In baptism the Lord is adding to our number
> those whom he is calling.
> People of God, will you welcome *these candidates*
> and uphold *them* in *their* new life in Christ?

To this, the people respond:

> With the help of God, we will.[4]

The service continues with questions to the candidate or their representatives about their commitment to Christ, concluding with this:

> Do you come to Christ, the way, the truth and the life?
> I come to Christ.[5]

The Anglican Communion is a body of people who have chosen to respond to Jesus' calling, and are on a shared journey, learning and celebrating and living the part each has been given to play.

If vocation starts with coming to Jesus, it continues by learning to understand where we are sent. Baptism is the first and fundamental response to the vocation to discipleship. Discipleship leads to ministry – this is a pattern we see over and again in scripture.

---

3 From the Vocations site of the Church of England. http://vocation-churchofengland.org/menu, accessed 12 September 2017.
4 www.churchofengland.org/prayer-worship/worship/texts/newpatterns/sampleservicescontents/npw7.aspx, accessed 23 May 2017.
5 http://vocation-churchofengland.org/menn/, accessed 25 March 2017.

CONFIRMATION

This next stage of our vocation is affirmed for Anglicans in confirmation, that celebration of an individual taking their place as a mature member, or minister, of the Church. Anglicans share with some other denominations the practice of confirmation. Confirmation is often understood simply in terms of a mature and responsible acceptance of, or owning, the decision made on an infant's behalf in baptism.

But the truth is much more exciting than that. It is the moment when a Christian steps up and says, "Count me in – now let me play my part," and the Church, on behalf of Christ, says, "Yes." It is the moment when the vocation to discipleship becomes the vocation to ministry, when the Church says, "Don't just be a follower *of* the team – now you get to play *in* the team."

In many places, the admission to Holy Communion is still linked to confirmation, and this can be seen as inviting the candidate to a seat at the table, to share in the meal to strengthen him or her in the ministry to which she or he is called.

In the confirmation service, candidates are expected to reaffirm the promises and commitments made at their baptism, but then the service continues with prayers for the Holy Spirit's equipping for Christian life and ministry:

> Almighty and ever-living God,
> you have given these your servants new birth
> in baptism by water and the Spirit,
> and have forgiven them all their sins.
> Let your Holy Spirit rest upon them:
> the Spirit of wisdom and understanding;
> the Spirit of counsel and inward strength;
> the Spirit of knowledge and true godliness;
> and let their delight be in the fear of the Lord.
> Amen.
>
> *The bishop addresses each candidate by name*
> N, God has called you by name and made you his own.
>
> *The bishop then lays a hand on the head of each, saying*
> Confirm, O Lord, your servant with your Holy Spirit.
> Amen.[6]

6 www.churchofengland.org/media/44650/7bce.html, accessed 23 May 2017.

Anglicans across the world share this understanding. Here's how the Episcopal Church of the United States of America puts the same prayer:

> Almighty God, we thank you that by the death and resurrection of your Son Jesus Christ you have overcome sin and brought us to yourself, and that by the sealing of your Holy Spirit you have bound us to your service. Renew in *these* your *servants* the covenant you made with *them* at *their* Baptism. Send *them* forth in the power of that Spirit to perform the service you set before *them*; through Jesus Christ your Son our Lord, who lives and reigns with you and the Holy Spirit, one God, now and for ever. Amen.[7]

These words, for the equipping of the Holy Spirit for life and ministry, are strikingly similar to those which are said at an ordination service. That's because every Christian has a vocation, a part to play in growing the kingdom of God, which they undertake as members of the Church, part of the team.

This vocation to ministry can take many different forms, from a calling to intercede at home, or make tea after a church service. It may be to volunteering roles in the community, or a profession, or a role in a family, a church, or the world.

George Herbert, one of the best-known Anglican writers, wrote a wonderful hymn which sums this up beautifully:

> Teach me, my God and King,
> in all things thee to see,
> and what I do in anything
> to do it as for thee.

Our whole lives are to be an expression of vocation – lived in obedient response to the call of God.

Vocation in the Church or in the world? – the context of vocation for Anglicans

It is often said that Anglicanism constantly has "a foot in both camps". It is Catholic *and* Reformed, it offers vocation to both priests and people – and

---

7 *The 1979 U.S. Book of Common Prayer: Formatted.* http://justus.anglican.org/resources/bcp/confirm.pdf, accessed 4 June 2017.

it sends people into both the Church and into the world. Anglicanism is rooted in its geographical and social context. It was born out of a desire to frame a national Church that would offer a context for worship and ministry which would embrace an entire nation – England. This was a church whose boundaries, as someone has said, were defined not so much by doctrine as by sea – a Church which was everywhere and for everyone. Of course Anglicanism is now much wider than simply the Church of England – but that history continues to shape it, with its concept of a "cure of souls" held by the local church for everyone residing in a parish, without exception. This means that a vocation for an Anglican will never simply be in the Church, but it will also be in the world. Anglicans do not withdraw from the world to live out their lives of discipleship to Jesus, but they discover and serve him in the world.

This can be frustrating for local clergy, some of whom would like nothing more than for their church members to be fully occupied filling the church rotas and committees. Meanwhile, for church members who just come to church once a week, perhaps at the eight o'clock, it can be a source of anxiety and guilt. But just as some are called to play a part in maintaining the life of the local church as a visible sign of God's presence in the midst of each community, so others are called to be out in those communities serving Jesus in many other ways.

So, the context of vocation for Anglicans may find itself in either *church* or in *kingdom*. They are not mutually exclusive, of course, and should certainly not be pitted against each other as if one were superior, or even as though Jesus might prefer one to the other – he came to found both, and his followers are called to both. But it may help identify our own individual vocations if we understand that our primary vocation may be lived out in the context of the Church, serving and building up the body of Christ – or in the kingdom, serving Christ and expressing the ministry of the body of Christ in the world.

Varieties of vocation in Anglicanism – "authorised" ministries

I hope it's clear by now that everyone in the Anglican Communion has a vocation. There is a genuine sense in which all vocations are to a "ministry of the Church", because *all* ministry is as part of the body of Christ. However, there are some ministries which are recognised and "authorised" – not just by an individual local parish, but by the wider Church. It is a great joy, but also a responsibility, to be affirmed in a calling to one of these authorised ministries, for which training (perhaps better understood as formation) is provided either locally or nationally. Each of these ministries bears a particular responsibility for keeping the Church "on track" in its calling to be the body of Christ – some by teaching, others by praying, or in other ways.

READER MINISTRY

Readers are not ordained, but are theologically trained and serve under licence to the bishop to preach, teach and offer pastoral care. They are often recognised as those who make a particular bridge between the Church and the world, and serve alongside parish clergy. They offer a vital role in strengthening the overall ministry of the Church.

CHURCH ARMY EVANGELISTS[8]

Church Army Evangelists are called and trained in mission, both in words and action, and they form teams to help others share in outreach often to those on the margins of society. They have fairly recently been re-formed into a "mission community within the Anglican Communion" with a particular focus on evangelism working within the UK and Ireland.

THE RELIGIOUS LIFE

Some men and women are called to live as celibate members of community, either apart from or immersed in the world, with a special commitment to prayer. Such communities have played a hugely significant part in the life of the Church at various points in history, and experienced a significant revival in the nineteenth century. Still important today, the common life is now also shared by some living in "new monastic communities" or "third orders", who may not have authorised ministries but are sustained in their Christian life and ministries by a common discipline.

ORDAINED MINISTRY

It may seem strange to arrive so late at ordination in this short chapter on vocation. After all, ordination was for many years considered the only true vocation – or at least the one that was superior to all others. The thrust of this chapter has been to challenge this misconception. But it would be wrong to undermine the vocation to ordination – after all, it has shaped my life. And those following this vocation shape the Church.

---

8 http://vocation.churchofengland.org/church-army-evangelist

The New Zealand prayer book puts it like this:

> We stand within a tradition
> in which there are deacons, priests and bishops.
> They are called and empowered to fulfil an ordained ministry
> and to enable the whole mission of the Church.
> Our authority is in Scripture
> and in the Church's continuing practice through the ages.[9]

The vocation to ordination for an Anglican can be to one of three orders of ministry – as a deacon, a priest, or a bishop. Their work is to "build up the Body of Christ in the Church to serve the world" through teaching, preaching, pastoral care and more.[10] The foundational order is as a deacon, the ministry of the one who is sent to serve.

> Deacons… are to proclaim the gospel in word and deed, as agents of God's purposes of love. They are to serve the community in which they are set, bringing to the Church the needs and hopes of all the people. They are to work with their fellow members in searching out the poor and weak, the sick and lonely and those who are oppressed and powerless, reaching into the forgotten corners of the world, that the love of God may be made visible… They are to be faithful in prayer, expectant and watchful for the signs of God's presence, as he reveals his kingdom among us.[11]

Some are called to the "distinctive diaconate" – to be a deacon is to fulfil their vocation. Others (the majority) are called to the diaconate within their calling to priesthood. For Anglicans, each of the three orders builds on the one before – so the vocation to priesthood is in truth a vocation to be a deacon and a priest, and similarly the vocation to being a bishop is a vocation as deacon, priest, and bishop. A bishop is called to the oversight of the Church, and to represent and guard her unity. A priest shares the servant ministry of a deacon, but is also given authority to represent the ministry of the Church committed to her by Jesus – a ministry of leadership and mission in which they are called to preside over the ministry of the sacraments – to absolve, to bless, to celebrate the Eucharist (Holy Communion).

> Priests are called to be servants and shepherds among the people to whom they are sent. With their Bishop and fellow ministers, they are to proclaim the word of the Lord and to watch for the signs of God's

---

9   A New Zealand Prayer Book: He Karakia o Aotearoa. http://anglicanprayerbook.nz/898.html, accessed 4 June 2017. Used with permission.

10 www..churchofengland.org/prayer-worship/worship/texts/ordinal/deacons.aspx, accessed 12 September 2017.

11 http://vocation.churchofengland.org/ordained-ministry

new creation. They are to be messengers, watchmen and stewards of the Lord; they are to teach and to admonish, to feed and provide for his family, to search for his children in the wilderness of this world's temptations, and to guide them through its confusions, that they may be saved through Christ for ever. Formed by the word, they are to call their hearers to repentance and to declare in Christ's name the absolution and forgiveness of their sins… Guided by the Spirit, they are to discern and foster the gifts of all God's people, that the whole Church may be built up in unity and faith.[12]

The priest does not directly represent Jesus Christ. This idea can lead to serious difficulties both for a priest and for the Church in which they serve, drawing unhelpful attention to the woman or man who is ordained. The priest represents the Church, and the Church represents Jesus Christ. Anglican ordination only happens for ministry in a particular place. You cannot be ordained without what is called a "title parish" – a priest's ministry without a parish context is meaningless. A priest represents the Church's ministry to the wider world, and also represents the Church's ministry to herself, always calling her back to her true vocation to be the body of Christ in the world. So, when a priest pronounces the words of the absolution, or the blessing, or the words of Jesus, at communion, they are speaking on behalf of the Church, which is speaking with the authority of Christ. It is an astonishing privilege, but one which only makes sense in the context of the vocation of the whole Church to be the body of Christ.

This is expressed beautifully in the liturgy of the Scottish Episcopal Church:

> The ministerial priesthood and the priesthood of all believers are related. Each in its proper way partakes of the one priesthood of Christ.[13]

The ministry of a priest or a deacon is a wonderful responsibility. It may be exercised full- or part-time, it may be paid or unpaid. It may be within a church or a chaplaincy context, but it is never in isolation from other Christians. The vocation to ordained ministry can help us to understand the vocation of all baptised Christians – those who make up the Church. Just as a priest represents the ministry of the Church, so all Christians together make up the ministry of Christ in the world today.

---

12 For full texts see: www.churchofengland.org/prayer-worship/worship/texts/ordinal/priests.aspx.
    Extracts accessed 25 March 2017.
13 www.scotland.anglican.org/wp-content/uploads/2014/01/scottish-ordinal-1984.pdf, accessed 4 June 2017.

So, what's your vocation?

There are many books wholly devoted to this subject, and we cannot begin to do justice to the whole area here. However, discovering your life as a vocation is just too exciting for me not to give a couple of pointers and encouragements for those just stepping into this discovery, or rediscovering it afresh. Firstly, it's important to talk to others. Anglican vocation is always vocation within the context of the Church and the world, and can only be understood in relation to others, so you just can't work out your vocation by yourself.

I used to be a Diocesan Director of Ordinands. It was my job to talk to people who were considering a vocation to ordained ministry in the Anglican Communion. One of the key sets of questions asked of these potential ordinands was this: "Is your vocation realistic, informed and obedient?" I used to put the questions up in a presentation against a beautiful picture of the Christ the Redeemer above the bay in Rio de Janeiro – because it was a way of helping us remember "RIO" – our three key questions. They are not just good questions for those sensing a call to ordained ministry – these are good questions for anyone considering any calling.

As you try to discern what you are called to, ask first if it is realistic. That's really about whether you are actually cut out for the role you aspire to. If you want to lead the singing in church but you are tone deaf, you are probably mistaken about what God is calling you to do. If you want to be a steeplejack but are scared of heights, it's probably not your vocation. If you have a real sensitivity for the emotions of others and find yourself instinctively drawing close to them in times of joy or sorrow, and you have some time at your disposal, you may well be called to a ministry of pastoral care. If you have a shrewd head for figures and the opportunity to search for a new job, perhaps you are called to work as an accountant, maybe for a charity.

Secondly, is your sense of vocation informed? Sometimes men or women would come to see me very sure that they were called to ordination, but with little idea of what that actually means. Invest some time in researching the possible role – find out everything you can about it, and as you do you will get a better feel as to whether it's actually for you.

Thirdly, and most importantly, is it obedient? A vocation is a calling. It's not a bright idea which has simply emerged in your own head. In testing a sense of vocation, it's vital to look for signs that this is Jesus' call to you.

That can come in many different ways, including dreams and visions, but more often through the insights of others who know you well. When someone says, "I could see you doing…", or, "Have you ever thought of …?" it may be a sign of vocation.

Called to be… called to do!

The fundamental vocation for Anglicans, as for all Christians, is to be conformed to Christ. A wise man once said to me, "Always remember that what God wants to do *in* you is more significant than what God wants to do *through* you." This little sentence continues to serve me well, as each day I seek to be open to what God is doing in me, before wondering what God wants to do through me. Rowan Williams, whose little book *Silence and Honey Cakes* remains my favourite of all books on vocation, speaks in that book of meeting Jesus in heaven and being asked not, "Why weren't you Martin Luther King, or Mother Teresa?" but, "Why weren't you Rowan Williams?"[14]

The joy of vocation for an Anglican is the possibility to be yourself, to play your part and see God glorified and God's kingdom extended, in the Church and in the world. That makes life worth living.

---

14 Rowan Williams, *Silence and Honey Cakes* (Oxford: Lion, 2003), 95.

The Joy of the Prayer Book for an Anglican

by the Revd Dr Daniel Newman

Daniel grew up in Dorset and read medicine at Oxford, before training for ordination at Ridley Hall, Cambridge. He returned to Dorset to serve as Assistant Curate at St John's Church, Weymouth, before becoming the Assistant Minister at St John's Woking. He is a member of the Group for Renewal of Worship and a trustee of the Prayer Book Society. He is married to Brooke and they have four children: Cædmon, Jerome, Reuben and Anastasia. He enjoys early music, the novels of P. G. Wodehouse, Dorothy Sayers and John Buchan, exploring the English countryside and discovering new loose-leaf teas.

Discovering the Book of Common Prayer has contributed significantly to my being an Anglican today. I didn't grow up in a churchgoing family, although I heard the Gospel and started to learn what it meant to be a Christian through the midweek children's groups at my parish church. During my teenage years, I went to non-Anglican churches with a school friend and his family.

One Wednesday afternoon in the sixth form after coming home from playing squash, I turned on the radio and heard a choir. As I listened, I was gradually able to make out what they were singing. I opened my Bible and was excited to discover that I could pretty much follow the words exactly – they were chanting the psalms! I had tuned in to Choral Evensong. As I kept listening, I heard readings from the Bible. I somehow knew that my mother had a Prayer Book, so I took it out of her wardrobe and discovered that the choir had sung other parts of scripture as well – the Magnificat and the Nunc Dimittis.

It was at university that I had my first "live" experience of Choral Evensong, and by my final year it was a regular fixture on Friday evenings, as part of my wooing of the girl who is now my wife.

In the Church of England's canons, Canon A5 identifies the Book of Common Prayer as one of the places in which the Church of England's doctrine is to be found. When I was ordained and licensed I had to affirm my loyalty to the inheritance of faith, of which the Book of Common Prayer is a part, as my inspiration and guidance under God in bringing the grace and truth of Christ to this generation and making him known to those in my care.

But the Prayer Book is not just something that I have to use, but something I get to use. I find C. S. Lewis' apologetic for old books equally applicable to liturgy. He compares a diet of predominantly new books to joining a conversation at the end and failing to get a joke because it relies on knowledge of what has been said before. Modern books also tend to reinforce what we already believe, for good and ill. Reading old books, including liturgy, is like checking one's blind spot to make sure one hasn't missed anything which might get one into trouble or hurt others.

> The only palliative is to keep the clean sea breeze of the centuries blowing through our minds, and this can only be done by reading old books. Not, of course, that there is any magic about the past. People were no cleverer than they are now; they made as many mistakes as we. But not the same mistakes. They will not flatter us in the errors we are already committing; and their own errors, being now open and palpable, will not endanger us.[1]

1 C. S. Lewis, "Introduction", in St Athanasius, *On the Incarnation* (Crestwood, NY: St Vladimir's Seminary Press, 1993), 5.

Reformation scholar Ashley Null sums up Thomas Cranmer's understanding of the human person in these oft-quoted words: "What the heart loves, the will chooses, and the mind justifies." This suffuses the Prayer Book, for which Cranmer is still largely responsible, even following the revisions that took place in the sixteenth and seventeenth century, after his martyrdom. For me, a large part of the joy of the Prayer Book for an Anglican is that it contains what Null calls Thomas Cranmer's "Gospel of Divine Allurement".

Morning and Evening Prayer

The trend has been observed that the future generation of leaders can be increasingly found at Choral Evensong.[2] Chaplains of Oxford and Cambridge Colleges are suggesting that students value the opportunity to escape the constant daily bombardment of information and sit in silence at the end of a hard day's work. There is, of course, the range of beautiful musical settings of Prayer Book texts spanning centuries. Even those who aren't committed Christians, including atheists and people of other religions, are finding a welcome, perhaps because the pressure to express a mature Christian commitment isn't an integral part of the service, and are coming to faith.

The Offices begin with sentences of scripture inviting us to acknowledge and turn away from our sins, and they are full of God's gracious character. Beginning with confession of sin is humbling. I am not claiming to be a good person but I am admitting that I am not – there is no room for pride. The introduction tells us "that we should not dissemble nor cloke" our sins from God, and it is remarkably freeing in a culture where we constantly feel the pressure to conceal our flaws and give the impression that we are successful, that we do not have to pretend before God.

When I confess my sins with other people, including the people along the row at whom I look out of the corner of my eye, and whom I think have everything together, that takes away reason for any despair I might feel. I do not save up all my sins until I say the Confession. As the Prayer Book tells us, "We ought at all times humbly to acknowledge our sins before God." Instead, it reminds me of who I am, so I give thanks and praise for what God has done for me, listen to God's word, and pray in recognition that I still need to change.

Part of the beauty of the Prayer Book Confession is the concrete, visual language, some of which even children can comprehend: "We have erred

---

2 John Bingham, "Looking for Britain's Future Leaders? Try Evensong", *The Telegraph* (1 March 2016). www.telegraph.co.uk/news/religion/12176998/Looking-for-Britains-future-leaders-Try-evensong.html, accessed 24 May 2017.

and strayed from thy ways like lost sheep." The Confession diagnoses that the source of my problem is the desires of my heart and that I am guilty of both sins of omission and commission. When I say, "And there is no health in us," I am admitting that I cannot save myself, and when I describe myself as a "miserable offender", I am acknowledging my need of mercy. I plead for mercy on the basis of God's "promises declared unto mankind in Christ Jesu our Lord," and I am assured that God "pardoneth and absolveth all them that truly repent and unfeignedly believe his holy Gospel".

The Confession and Absolution were new from 1552. It is hard to imagine how it would have felt to have heard for the first time that it is possible to have direct access to God through Jesus Christ, confess our sins, have assurance of forgiveness, and not to have to go around burdened by the guilt of our sins until we next confess them to a priest and perform the prescribed penance. As one who has been forgiven, I am adopted as one of God's children and can call him "Father", which I do in the words of the Lord's Prayer.

I was first drawn to the Prayer Book when I heard the text of Coverdale's Psalms set simply but beautifully to music using Anglican chant, and I continue to value the way the Prayer Book helps me regularly to pray through the psalms. Dietrich Bonhoeffer said:

> Whenever the Psalter is abandoned, an incomparable treasure is lost to the Christian Church. With its recovery will come unexpected power.[3]

The psalms contrast our mortality and sinfulness with God's eternity, and portray a God who does not abandon sinful people but is gracious and forgiving. They reflect on God's redemption of Israel and promise to bless the world through a king from the nation. The psalms present a God who chooses to dwell amongst human beings and they allow us to glimpse a place of refuge, justice and abundance which God will one day establish, while giving voice to the pain of life in a world where this is not yet experienced and often opposed. The psalms delight in God's physical creation and sustaining of it, while acknowledging the presence of chaos within it, and eagerly awaiting God's coming to put everything right. The psalms rejoice in the treasure of God's word and present God, and not just God's gifts, as the one whom we should desire.

Jesus and his earliest followers would have sung and prayed the psalms and understood his identity as God's king and the key elements of his mission – his suffering, death, resurrection and ascension – in the light of them.

---

3 Cited in Eric Metaxas, *Bonhoeffer: Pastor, Martyr, Prophet, Spy* (Nashville, TN: Thomas Nelson, 2010), 368-369.

The psalms can help us to recover two particular forms of prayer. The first is lament. This is an antidote to a form of belief which imperturbably accepts God's will and implies that the Christian life should be one of continual victory, which leaves contemporary Christianity ill-equipped to deal with tragedy on a personal or a global level. The psalmists lament in a range of circumstances – opposition, betrayal, persecution, deprivation of health, the loss of material goods and isolation. Some end with no hope at all, yet even bringing one's complaint before God at such times is an expression of faith.

The second form of prayer the psalms can teach us is imprecation – praying for God to act in judgement. We can pray for the defeat of our spiritual enemies of the world, the flesh and the devil. Imprecatory prayers can be a response to opposition to God, God's chosen king and good purposes for the world – not just personal grievances. They assume a position in which our perspective is aligned with God's. They are not intended to satisfy resentment and vindictiveness as a reaction to private injury. We see the same behaviour in the New Testament in the cry of the martyrs under the altar in heaven in Revelation 6:10.[4]

Following the psalms comes the First Lesson, which charts the course of the creation of the world, its fallen condition, and the outworking of God's promise to bless the world in the history of Israel and her kings through conquest, exile and return. At Evening Prayer the Magnificat helps me rejoice with Mary that God keeps his promises in anticipation of the birth of Christ.

Then follows the Second Lesson, which narrates the life of Christ in the Gospels and expounds and applies it in the New Testament letters. The New Testament Lesson is followed by the Nunc Dimittis at Evening Prayer. Since, like Simeon, I see for myself that salvation has come in Christ, I can depart in peace and die the little death of sleep. Nothing need trouble my conscience. There is nothing of which I need to be afraid for the future. I then declare the faith that is revealed in the scriptures from creation to new creation.

The Prayer Book also teaches me how to pray for myself and others. Jesus' disciples asked him to teach them to pray and I am no different. Although prayer may be instinctive for me as a human being, I am prone to making God in my own image. My own tendency is simply to list requests with no emotional engagement with God, and my petitions often circle around the same narrow set of concerns, which reflect my priorities and not God's.

---

4 For more on the psalms, see Tom Wright, *Finding God in the Psalms: Sing, Pray, Live* (London: SPCK, 2014). For more on lament specifically, see Timothy Keller, *Walking with God through Pain and Suffering* (London: Hodder & Stoughton, 2013), 240-254.

For others, prayer may be almost exclusively an emotional experience, sensing the presence or love of God, with little or no cognitive content. In traditions where spontaneous prayer is valued, it is easy to fall into the same speech patterns and become repetitive, employing the ubiquitous "just", or using "God" as a punctuation mark at the end of a sentence. It is also easy slip into heresy by starting to address one person of the Trinity and subconsciously switching to another: "We just thank you for dying on the cross, Father God."

I came across a meme on the internet entitled, "If we talked to people the way we talk to God":

> Babe, could you just, just pick up some milk babe, while you're at the store? Just go ahead, babe, and just, just go to the milk section babe. Just grab a pint of milk and just, just place it right in your cart. Babe, just thanks, babe. Just.[5]

I do not find using the Prayer Book is opposed to *ex tempore*, spontaneous, prayer, but it is like playing jazz (so I am told). To improvise well, you need to put in a lot of practice first and learn about scales, harmonies and rhythm. If you try and improvise straight away, it will sound terrible.

Christian prayer is a verbal response to prior revelation of God's character and will, without bypassing either the reason or the emotions, which is possible because of Jesus' death on the cross to take away sins. I find the Prayer Book collects in particular teach me to pray by helping me better understand God and myself and what it means to live in the world. Collects are an ancient form of prayer that gather up the prayers of the congregation and are said on their behalf. They follow the same basic pattern with variations:

1. Address: who we ask – a name of God
2. Doctrine: why we can ask – a truth about God
3. Petition: what we want – the request
4. Aspiration: what we will do with it if we get it – the deeper prayer
5. In Jesus' name: how we can ask – remembering Jesus' mediation

Just this past week, I have been praying one of my favourite collects, the Collect of the Fourth Sunday after Easter which illustrates this:

5 "If we talked to people the way we talk to God". http://adam4d.com/lord-just, accessed 24 May 2017.

[Address]O Almighty God,

[Doctrine]who alone canst order the unruly wills and affections of sinful men:

[Petition]Grant unto thy people that they may love the thing which thou commandest, and desire that which thou dost promise;

[Aspiration]that so, among the sundry and manifold changes of the world, our hearts may surely there be fixed, where true joys are to be found;

[Mediation of Christ]through Jesus Christ our Lord.

This collect tells us that we are sinful human beings and the root problem is our disordered loves. We love the wrong things or we love good things but disproportionately. The fall hasn't just affected our emotions and left our reason intact – sin has also corrupted our will, the faculty by which we process information and make decisions about how we will act. What we need is a reordering of our loves – to love what God commands and desire what God promises. Our hearts need to be captured with true joys, the joys of the age to come, instead of the ephemeral things which this unstable world can offer, but which will ultimately let us down. Only God is able to do that work in our hearts and minds.

The two other collects at Morning and Evening Prayer remind us of the reality that we have enemies, including spiritual enemies, and we need God to defend us and keep us from danger. We need that both as we head out into the day and also at the end of the day – night-time is dangerous. The Prayer Book expands the subjects beyond that for which I would naturally pray. It gives me prayers I can reach for in a variety of circumstances and keeps me from forgetting to be thankful. I am encouraged to pray for the Queen, the royal family and the Church. Writing shortly after many, including children, were killed or injured by a terrorist attack at a concert and the threat level is critical, I can pray: "Save and deliver us, we humbly beseech thee, from the hands of our enemies; abate their pride, assuage their malice, and confound their devices."

The Litany, too, is apt at such a time: "From all sedition, privy conspiracy, and rebellion… Good Lord, deliver us." The Litany enumerates the sins, temptations and dangers from which I need to ask God for deliverance and teaches me the priority of praying for God to give us hearts to hear and receive the word and amend our lives in accordance with it. The Litany identifies a variety for whom I would not ordinarily seek God's providential care: "all that travel by land or by water, all women labouring of child, all sick persons, and young children"; "all prisoners and captives"; "the fatherless children, and widows, and all that are desolate and oppressed". The Litany reminds me that I need to look to God "to give and preserve to our use the kindly fruits of the earth, so as in due time we may enjoy them" and not to take them for granted.

I have written largely in the first person, but from 1552 onwards, Morning and Evening Prayer were intended for corporate use. We need to remind each other of God's character, tell each other afresh the story of salvation, weep and rejoice with one another in our present experience, and learn to pray together. It has been a source of particular joy to use the Prayer Book with my young family and witness my children start to learn the Confession, the Creed, the Lord's Prayer, and a few canticles and collects as we say (or sometimes sing) them.

The Lord's Supper

Dom Gregory Dix famously described the Communion Service in the Prayer Book as "The only effective attempt ever made to give liturgical expression to the doctrine of 'justification by faith alone.'" Participants follow the steps which, according to Cranmer, led to conversion of the will, renewed affections, repentance, and new life in Christ.[6]

First comes the Law, in the form of the Ten Commandments, which bring the recognition that we stand in need of God's mercy for transgressing them and the gracious work of the Holy Spirit in our hearts if we are to be able to keep them. Secondly comes the Gospel, as the word of God is read in the epistle and Gospel, synthesised in the Nicene Creed and expounded in the sermon. This is followed by the Prayer for the Church Militant, which includes the petition for grace to receive God's word effectively. Repentance is modelled by the Confession which follows. It recognises that God is our maker and judge and explores the nature of our sin as "manifold" (i.e. many and varied), "from time to time" (repeated), "by thought, word, and deed", and "against thy Divine Majesty" (a form of rebellion against our king). We are honest about the consequences of our sin ("provoking most justly thy wrath and indignation against us"), express repentance and sorrow, and admit that we cannot bear our sins

---

6 I am indebted to the schema outlined in Ashley Null, *Thomas Cranmer's Doctrine of Repentance: Renewing the Power to Love* (Oxford: OUP, 2000), 244-245.

ourselves and need someone else to bear them for us ("the burden of them is intolerable"). In the light of this we pray to our Father for mercy, forgiveness and grace to live new lives pleasing to him, which bring God honour and glory.

Following Confession we receive assurance of forgiveness in the Absolution and Comfortable Words – words that are full of comfort. Jesus says to those who feel burdened by all sorts of things – living for the approval of others, trying to keep God's commands, conscious of sin which we have just admitted – "Come... and I will refresh you." God loves us and we see that love demonstrated by sending the Son. And why? So that we should not perish but have everlasting life. Although we are sinners Jesus did not come to condemn us but save us. When we do sin, Jesus speaks to the Father on behalf and says, as it were, "Forgive them. My death on the cross was the sacrifice which turned aside the wrath they deserved because of their sins."

It is fairly axiomatic in our society that many of our problems are due to low self-esteem – mental illness, poor behaviour, addiction, joining gangs, crime. The solution that is often proposed is to boost our self-esteem, and this is reflected in the school curriculum. One of the reasons people state that they do not like the Prayer Book is the way it talks about sin and the need for repentance – this is felt to be harmful. It is right that we should not go around with an unhealthily low view of ourselves. Trying to correct that by telling ourselves and each other that we are valuable might sometimes be helpful in the short term, but it cannot ultimately work. Why should I believe myself or you when you tell me that I am valuable? If I get my sense of self-worth from anything I do – my achievements, my relationships – then where does that leave me when I fail or a relationship ends? Anyone who thinks that the Prayer Book encourages an unhealthily low view of ourselves (so-called "worm theology") has not spent enough time meditating on the Comfortable Words. Yes, I am a sinner, but I get my sense of worth from the fact that Jesus still invites me to come to him and that I know he died for me.

The next step after being convicted by the Law and responding to the Gospel in repentance and faith is re-entry into God's presence. The Sursum Corda bids us, "Lift up your hearts." Left in our natural condition we are weighed down by our sins and nothing could lift us from earth to heaven. But having heard the good news preached to us by Cranmer, I barely need to be told – how could my heart fail to be drawn upwards to God? We join in with the song of the heavenly throne room in the Sanctus. In the Prayer of Humble Access, we *do* presume to come to the Lord's Table, not "trusting in our own righteousness", but in God's "manifold and great mercies" and the constancy of God's character. God is "the same Lord whose property is always to have mercy". We claim Jesus' promise in John 6:53-56, of eating his body and drinking his blood by faith when we eat the bread and drink the wine in order to receive the benefits of his sacrificial death – cleansing and mutual indwelling.

The Prayer of Consecration itself describes Jesus' death as "redemption" (paying the price that sets us free from our sins and their consequences), an "oblation" (sacrificial offering) and "satisfaction" (meeting the requirements of the totality of God's character – God's justice and love). It emphasises the sufficiency of Jesus' death by its mention of his making "by his one oblation of himself once offered a full, perfect, and sufficient sacrifice, oblation, and satisfaction, for the sins of the whole world". Reception of the bread and wine immediately follows the words of institution – communion, not consecration, is the climax of the liturgy.

The final step is reception of power for a renewed holiness. We pray in the Lord's Prayer that we will forgive others because we have received afresh God's forgiveness in Christ. We offer our grateful service in the post-communion prayers. In the Gloria we praise God and acknowledge our ongoing dependence on God's mercy. Ashley Null sums up Cranmer's legacy in the Prayer Book thus: "At last grateful love clearly flowed from grateful love."[7]

Language

Although I have focused predominantly on theology, a further part of the joy of the Prayer Book is the language in which this theology comes. Features of Cranmer's masterful prose include alliteration and doubling (e.g. "devices and desires"), repetition of pronouns ("We have erred... We have followed... We have offended... We have left undone... We have done") and conjunctions (We have done this *and* we have done that *and* this is what we are like), and its rhythm.[8] Although traditional language is equated with formality, it offers the potential for intimacy which modern language denies us: we can address God as "Thou", which is an intimate form of address like the French *"tu"*.[9]

When I sit in Evensong, stand at the Lord's Table, or kneel at my prayer desk, as I smell the scents that come wafting on the clean sea breeze of the centuries, the Prayer Book woos me afresh for God.

---

7 Null, *Thomas Cranmer's Doctrine of Repentance*, 243.
8 My attention was drawn to these features by Alan Jacobs, *The Book of Common Prayer: A Biography* (Princeton, NJ: Princeton University Press, 2013), 61-63.
9 I am grateful for this insight to Brian Cummings (ed.), *The Book of Common Prayer: The Texts of 1549, 1559, and 1662* (Oxford: OUP, 2011), 692.

The Joy of Service
for an Anglican

by the Revd Victor and Evangelist Nolavy Osoro

Victor and Nolavy Osoro live and work in the Diocese of Toliara, in the south of Madagascar. Victor is originally from Kenya, and has served as a missionary for nine years – four of those as a parish priest. Nolavy graduated with a bachelor's degree in divinity and is the first Anglican woman in Madagascar to have a degree in theology. She is currently serving as the diocesan Children's Ministry Coordinator and parish evangelist, and at the same time preparing for ordination. When she is ordained, she will become the first woman to be ordained in Toliara.

Victor and Nolavy were married four years ago and have a three-year-old daughter, Fitahiana (the Malagasy word for "blessing"), and a baby son, Mshindi (the Swahili word for "winner").

Victor Osoro

In my church in Kenya we had two full-time clergy, three part-time clergy and around five lay readers. When I started working in this area in Madagascar there were only three full-time clergy and a handful of lay readers covering a thousand-mile stretch of coastline. I reckoned there was great need here – and that's when the Lord impressed upon my heart the call to serve as a missionary.

When I arrived, I worked with the youth and at the same time I was learning the language. I could see hearts that had a longing to be filled and a desire to learn, and I knew that was a good place to start. During the time we worked with them we had regular training, conferences and Bible studies. That strengthened people's spiritual muscles and, over time, people have grown to become more responsible. As a musician, I also trained a few of the young people in playing the synthesiser – and gosh, their skill now has surpassed me! I am thrilled to see that.

It was interesting to note that my not mastering the language did not stop or deter the young people from approaching me at any time to ask for direction and advice. The youth leadership was struggling at the time but now, after years of discipleship and training, they are able to stand on their own two feet, organise their ministry activities and accomplish them successfully. One of the young guys I trained then is now doubling up as a catechist and the diocesan youth president. It brings me so much joy to see people I have mentored grow in faith, become strong pillars in ministry and take up key leadership roles in the Church.

For the last four years I have been a parish priest in Mahabo parish, which has nine churches scattered across a geographical area covering around a hundred and ten miles to the east and a hundred and thirty-five miles to the west. There was no resident priest in Mahabo for about three years before I arrived, and I was the first priest to live in the parish headquarters. My coming to this parish answered the prayers that the Christian community had been praying for several years. The joy on their faces could not be hidden on the day of my installation – it was a relief for many, because they felt that their time to go to the next level in service and spirituality had come, since there would be close supervision and pastoral oversight.

The size of the congregation can range from fifteen people in the smallest to around a hundred and twenty adults in the larger congregations, and the total number of children in the parish is around five hundred. I manage to visit most of the churches once or twice a month. One is situated in a region that can't be reached by car, only motorbike. It's in a rice-growing area, so to get there I walk two or three miles through paddy fields in water up to my knees. I can't wear shoes and have to go barefoot. The walk through the rice fields takes me about an hour. I manage to do this journey about twice a month and I'm quite used to it. As I walk I am aware of the Christians who are waiting expectantly for me at the other side of the paddy fields, eager to learn from the Lord through God's servant.

One of the other churches is so remote that I manage to get there only about once or twice a year. The journey is a hundred and ten miles, which takes a good eight or nine hours' drive through the jungle, given the poor state of the road. There are eleven rivers to cross on this journey and no bridges so, when the rains come, no vehicle can get there. It means that the route is open for only four months, between August and November, and remains closed the rest of the time.

There are other dangers apart from the weather. Most of the houses in the area where one of our churches is situated have been torched and the Christians have moved to another village and worship in our other church there. Occasionally we are warned about cattle rustlers in the area, but by God's grace I haven't encountered any dangerous situations.

When I do get there, most of the people I meet are hungry for the Gospel and overjoyed to have direction and guidance. People take their mission seriously – to pass on the word of God to other people in their community. I remember at one time, when we were studying the Bible, I asked how many books there are in the Bible. An elderly woman stood up and said, "I have no idea how many they are but I just want to worship God and that's why I am here. Period." This reveals the zeal within her heart to be a disciple of Christ. So I would say that there is a lot of joy in serving people in this way.

For me, service is about pouring out your whole self – the giving of oneself fully and totally to the people you serve. You can't hold anything back, but it means sacrifice, humility, and a readiness to serve all people in all ways, in all things. I try to serve the churches and communities I work in, and in turn I see the people serving one another. There is a high level of poverty and life is hard, so in these farming communities people get together to help one another. They may come together to plant or harvest rice. For example, when a new church building is needed, the Christians join forces to build it. The end result will be a simple building, about ten metres by eight, with mud walls and a roof of corrugated iron or rice-straw thatch.

But as a place where God is worshipped it is no different from the grandest, most ornate cathedral.

In one of our churches, which is forty-five kilometres away from the parish headquarters, the Christians had been worshipping on the veranda of the catechist's house and felt that the time was right to build a temporary structure. Once the land was acquired, they had to make a plea and call on the women to fetch water, and the men to collect the wood required to complete the building and ferry it to the site by ox-cart, while other people began designing the structure. It took forty-six days to complete the work. It was great to see how everyone was committed to doing something. Those who could not fetch water would cook food for the builders. Wow! Is that not service from the bottom of the heart?

I would say that in each area around a quarter of the people know Christ, so there is a lot of work still to do. In each church there are lay ministers, catechists and evangelists. I am responsible for training the believers and equipping them to do the work, because I would not be able to do it all alone. We have sent several evangelists for training and we have one in his second year of training for ordination. It has been awesome to see how fast they have learnt the skills of outreach and discipleship, and have become wonderful teachers and preachers. And, in turn, they disciple others to do the same for Christ.

As a priest, one of my roles is to bring life to the liturgy of our churches, so that the words and the sacrament strengthen and sustain people for the weeks or months that lie ahead, until I am able to see them again. During that time people's faith may be tested by the extreme poverty in which most of them live, or by illness or natural disaster. When such times come, and they do come, I strongly believe that in whatever hardship they face, they will serve one another in faith.

Once, the house where one of our evangelists lived with his family was partly destroyed by a cyclone. I was amazed at the love people showed in helping in the reconstruction of the house. Under the leadership of the parish chair, people were able to gather all the items needed without requiring any finances from the parish account, which was negative at that time. Once the material was gathered, all the builders worked hard to complete the house. The lack in this region is so evident, but so is the joy that people have, and their zeal to serve both the Lord and their neighbour.

When I recite the Dismissal at the end of the liturgy, I am conscious that it may be weeks or months before I will be able to visit again. So it has particular resonance for me to say:

> The peace of God,
> which passes all understanding,
> keep your hearts and minds
> in the knowledge and love of God,
> and of his Son Jesus Christ our Lord;
> and the blessing of God almighty,
> the Father, the Son, and the Holy Spirit,
> be among you and remain with you always.

Then I say:

> Go in peace to love and serve the Lord.

And the people reply:

> In the name of Christ. Amen.

This part of the liturgy, for me, affirms that the word of God is not merely confined within the building that has been built out of mud and rice-straw thatch. I know that the people will take it out in their hearts and souls, to serve their community. In this way I serve people who, in turn, go on to serve others. And this, for me, sums up the joy of service for an Anglican.

Nolavy Osoro

I am of Malagasy descent. As a young girl I had the desire to serve the Lord, but unfortunately there was no one to give me the necessary training that I needed. The church leaders that I was to look up to seemed to be having endless conflicts and had very little time to concentrate on other matters.

I was the first child to give my life to Christ in our family. My father was the shaman: he came to Christ and gave up his tools weeks before he died in 2016.

I thank God that the Lord brought a wonderful lady to my life as a mentor who spent time with me and shared with me truths and opened her heart to me. We spent a lot of time praying and studying God's word together. That, I must say, has contributed a lot to my life and has shaped much of what I am today. When the Lord called me to ministry I was a little hesitant, not knowing what my dad would make of it. I had to talk to my spiritual mentor, who later shared my situation with the bishop. To my surprise, the bishop invited my parents to his house, just a stone's throw from our house, and had a one-to-one meeting with them about me and the call in my life.

What happened next was the beginning of a new path in my spirituality. My dad, of all people, entrusted my spiritual life and calling to the bishop, with no idea where that would lead. He said that what he did as the shaman should by no means be a stumbling block to my quest to serve the Lord. But, he said, given the nature of his occupation, he would not be much help to me in terms of giving me direction and spiritual support. I was stunned. I had not seen this coming. I received this news with great delight and I knew in my heart that it was a beginning of a new era.

Later, the Lord spoke to me through dreams, and three dreams in particular catapulted me to the next level. These dreams did not happen concurrently but at different times, when I was at different ages.

I was barely twelve in the first dream. In that dream, I saw a child crying and running away from a man who was chasing him. The man was carrying a machete and was after the young boy's blood. He clearly saw every turn this boy made and was on his neck. It appeared that the boy was running from home and that his parents too were helpless and could not stop this man from chasing their child. I got so worried and wondered in my heart who could rescue this young man. Looking at myself, naïve and young, I knew there was nothing much that I could do. While I looked around, I discovered that all the people around were watching him and did not seem to act. It did not look serious to them.

The second dream was about a tree on fire. Everybody who saw the fire did not dare to move closer, but tried to find excuses not to approach the tree, which was in the church compound. When I came forward, they tried to convince me not to approach the tree because the fire was too fierce. I did not listen to them, but continued on my way and approached the tree. When I drew closer, I climbed up and saw several sections underground that had scary animals and skulls inside and, interestingly, the blazing flames slowly died back. I then walked courageously past the people along a very narrow path that would easily scare other people. But I neither got burnt nor fell into the scary ditch.

Some time later I had a third dream. In this dream I saw a child who had fallen in a well and was in great need of help. He cried out to me and asked me to pull him out. When I tried pulling him out, I realised that I did not have the strength. As I wondered what to do next, I turned and looked up, and saw Jesus standing at a nearby tree. At the sight of him I received a special strength and I was able to pull the boy out with ease. The joy on the boy's face could not be hidden. He said, "You have saved me, you have saved me!" In awe, I told him that I was not the one who had saved him: it was actually the Lord himself.

These dreams spoke to me a lot. In a sense God was revealing himself to me and sending me to be of help to the many people in our society who were in the well, or running away desperate for help, or afraid of flames – starting with my family, and especially the children around us. The poverty and everyday struggles that my people go through are so overwhelming that you just get drained by looking at them and realising that you don't have the energy to do nearly as much as you would like to. I mean, you get discouraged even before you start. With these dreams, the Lord encouraged me that it is from God that we draw our strength, and it is to God's glory to bring people out of the well, or to save them from the flames, or from a pursuer, and take them to a place of safety. That hit me hard.

Before I knew it, I was in training to become an evangelist so as to be better placed to serve and reach out to those who seek help. This I knew was not going to be easy. The Lord brought Isaiah to my mind, which gave me a lot of comfort:

> But now thus says the Lord, he who created you, O Jacob, he who formed you, O Israel: Do not fear, for I have redeemed you; I have called you by name, you are mine. When you pass through the waters, I will be with you; and through the rivers, they shall not overwhelm you; when you walk through fire you shall not be burned, and the flame shall not consume you.
>
> Isaiah 43:1-2

In due time, most of my family members, seeing what the Lord was doing in my life and how lives were being changed, also made a decision to receive Christ as Lord and Saviour! They have become so committed and some have leadership roles in the Church.

My call was to serve the children. And as things unfolded, after graduating from college I was appointed the first diocesan Children's Ministry Coordinator. It is in this service that I have come across children who have been left to themselves by their parents. Some have been molested, or sent by their parents into lives of prostitution to help make ends meet in the family, while others have had to work and study at the same time at a tender age; others are lured and bound by drugs, leading them to be pushers or addicts. I have had to face difficult people and make tough decisions to help these children.

On one occasion, I met a young girl who always seemed to keep to herself. Every time I met her, she seemed depressed and people seemed to avoid her, probably due to her occasional angry outbursts. I wondered what could be the problem. I took a step of faith and approached her to find out what was happening in her life. The first meeting with her obviously did not go well, because she felt that I was prying into her life. I stepped back a bit but I did not give up. I prayed for her and asked God for wisdom. I got to know when her birthday was and organised a surprise gift for her. I wrapped it well and put it in her room. And yes – that made the magic! The next time I came to see her, tears were rolling down her cheeks and she ran towards me and held me tightly as she mumbled the words "thank you" over and again. I was not sure what was going on. I gave her time to express her emotions. Afterwards, I sat down with her and she opened her heart and told me what was going on in her life:

> When I was a bit younger, my mother died. My father got another wife and he forgot about us completely. As I grew, I did not experience love of any kind. Life has been tough on me. My stepmother did nothing to help me. She actually chased us out of our house and my dad could not help us at all! I developed a strong hatred towards my dad and men in general. I saw men as irresponsible and careless. I then took up martial arts to learn defence techniques in case any man came near me and tried to hurt me. I also made a decision never to get married, given my view of how all men are just like my dad. That is what has kept me depressed for a long time, because I could not share this with anyone. Since my mum's death, I have felt that no one is out there who cares for me. And so I have been carrying this knife in my bag everywhere I go, ready to stab any man who crosses my path.

I took a deep breath as she brought the knife out: it had been tucked into her bikini. She paused, and said:

I am happy to know that there is someone who can show love to me. Someone who can listen to me without judging me. Someone, who has true concern about my concerns. A shoulder to lean on. Thank you, Nolavy.

I hugged her and we prayed together and I encouraged her with scripture, reassuring her that the Lord cares for us and that God's love for us is higher than the mountains. From that time onwards we began spending more time praying and studying God's word together. As time went by she became free and was able to interact with other people well. The Lord brought about the change in her life. The depression turned to laughter. She no longer walked around with a knife, but rather with a Bible. All bitterness in her life was turned to sweetness and she had a bright countenance. She met a wonderful man who asked her to marry him some time later and, as I write this, she is preparing for their wedding in the next few months. This is a totally changed life to the glory of God.

Seeing lives changed has always given me the joy of service. As I have seen this happen several times, I do not seem to have any fear within my heart, because I know that the Lord is on my side and will strengthen and help me to stand firm as I tread hard ground and face strong opposition and deal with difficult stuff in my ministry. And I realise that some of these are things that not everyone wants to become involved with. But with the Lord's hand upon me I will walk alone in such times and still be victorious in God's name.

The Joy of Prayer
for an Anglican

by Heather Smith

Heather Smith is a writer and editor, and was ordained priest in 2003. After spending most of her life in cities, she and her husband recently moved to a village in rural Wiltshire where she is enjoying the new adventure of country life. She has an interest in interfaith issues, particularly Islam and Christianity, and is currently working on a PhD in the subject. In her spare time Heather sings in a choir and, on sunny days, she and her husband like driving their elderly MX5 with the hood down.

I am not, to borrow a phrase, a cradle Anglican. Baptised a Presbyterian, I spent my formative years first in the United Reformed Church and later in the Church of Scotland. As a child and teenager, it seemed that prayer consisted of the words of an individual, or those written by the minister for a particular service. They were more along the lines of Anglican intercessions, with added thanksgiving and praise. I was not aware of any of the prayers I heard in a service being reused, but perhaps they were. I fear now that I am not doing them justice, but my journey was to lead me elsewhere. Of course we were encouraged to pray ourselves – to close our eyes and say what was in our hearts.

At my first Anglican service, as a young adult completely unfamiliar with Church of England liturgy, I, together with a fellow newcomer, reached for my purse when the priest announced "the collect for the day". The expression didn't sound quite right, but our best interpretation was that a collection was about to be taken up. I had a long way to go!

At that time, perhaps the most striking element of the service was the open invitation to communion. All who received communion in their own church were welcome. The idea drew me in to a new world where the prayers and liturgy were available to all and had seen people through the ups and downs of life for centuries. It was the eternal nature of the Church that interested me, with its bishops and priests ordained at the hands of other bishops who came before, reaching back in time.

Not long afterwards my niece was baptised. The service was in the Church of Scotland, but her grandmother, my sister-in-law's mother, was a staunch Church of England-goer. I bought a Bible as a christening present – small and white and, as it happened, about the size of the Book of Common Prayer.

"Is that a prayer book?" asked grandmother.

"Er, no, it's a Bible," I replied, wondering why on earth she thought I would buy my niece a prayer book.

It was only later that it occurred to me that the Book of Common Prayer, which I had by then come to know as a book of services, was, in fact, a prayer book, in the sense of being a book of prayers. I suppose the clue was in the name. So, logically speaking, the whole service must also count as a prayer. The old-fashioned formal language and set liturgy were a far cry from any understanding of prayer I had growing up, but what an interesting idea! Much later, a priest with whom I did a placement while at theological college used to invite me to join him in the Daily Office, with the words, "Let's say some prayers," and I remembered my epiphany over the Book of Common Prayer. "Yes," I thought, "let's".

Living in London as a young adult, the Church of England became my Sunday home. I grew to love the steady liturgy of the Alternative Service Book, and BCP Evensong, which I now understood as prayer, whether or not the words were prefaced by "Let us pray." I discovered that the words could mean something different according to my mood or circumstances, while also having the same meaning every time they were said.

I came to confirmation classes only after my second child was born. The inclusiveness of Anglicanism meant that I had never felt excluded because I was a member of another denomination. In the session on prayer, the priest suggested that we might like to write our own prayers. She meant by this not that we could write down the words we wanted to say in the moment, to address a transitory need or give thanks for a blessing just received – but a prayer that would last, like the collects or a prayer of St Francis of Assisi.

Obviously someone wrote the collects, and saints such as St Augustine wrote prayers which had passed down the centuries, but I had never thought that someone like me could write such a prayer – something I would say many times, which spoke of my faith, my relationship with God and of eternal things that mattered. Surely these prayers were for someone special to write – someone trained, or someone, well, saintly? Surprised at myself, I tried. Some I would keep for a while, but others seemed worth only one recitation, and then belonged in the bin. But there was something about writing them down. It seemed to emphasise the way in which they stayed in God's heart for ever – a heart that surely must be larger than we can ever imagine, keeping as it does all the prayers that men and women have prayed across the years. Our prayers and our lives, as they are, for ever in God's memory and for ever present in eternity.

When I spoke to a friend, a vicar's daughter, about my new-found love of these lasting prayers, she searched out and bought me a book of prayers for every day of the year. It included the prayers of saints and poets, the famous and not so famous, covering an array of subjects, many of which I would never have thought of myself. But how it enriched my prayer life and my understanding of God! I settled down to pray daily, with my new resources to share with God. And it was, or course, a short step to the Daily Office.

Much earlier, I had begun to sing in choirs. We sang the great masses of Mozart, Bach and Beethoven, along with other liturgical and devotional music by composers old and new. These too, I began to see as prayers. They sustained me in difficult times. My prayer to God was always present in the words and music of these great musicians. As we sang, our prayer rose to the throne of heaven. And surely it mattered little whether all the singers believed or not. It could not fail to reach, and whoever sang, even unconsciously, must be affected by God's reply of joy at all our efforts, returning our song in the blessings of the world around us, which seemed to increase in intensity of colour and sensation.

Finding the Daily Office, I began to take time with it every day. Here, too, I felt that sense of joining with others, as millions of Christians, in millions of different places, together or alone, took part in the daily rhythm of prayer. I had started to feel drawn to ordination. It seemed to explain me, and everything about me. It was as if I had been, all unknowingly, walking along a path to reach this Anglican place, when all would fit together. God had drawn me through experience and ever deeper prayer towards a place of service. But here as I pondered, the place that might seem the goal was only another new beginning, a step on the way which still had, and has, more to give.

I carefully spoke of ordination to the vicar. Encouragingly, he suggested I go and speak to a nun from whom he often sought spiritual direction.

"A nun?" I questioned in surprise. "You want me to go and see a nun? How do you do that exactly?"

He laughed. And so I went. "Do join us in the chapel at noon," said the Sister.

The silence in there was thick with meaning as we waited for the chapel bell to ring and the sweet ethereal voices singing the prayers that they sang every day of the year. Their song stretched out behind us into the past and forward into the future. It was as if time was suspended and we stood in eternity. And more, this prayer encompassed me. It invited me in. Not only was I welcomed by the Sisters, but how much more by God. I knew, of course, that prayer was not one way, an asking and bothering God with constant talking, but a two-way experience of communication. Here, I felt it very much – silenced as God welcomed and spoke in the words of the liturgy.

Later, after ordination, in my first parish, members of the ministry team met together to say Morning Prayer. Sometimes only two of us could be there – the full-timers who had the privilege of a stipend, allowing us to pass each day ministering in the parish. On other days we were joined by those who juggled other commitments. Here, as in the convent, we found God, but the bustling work in the parish gave our experience a feel of time out in a busy schedule, all that we did in our busy lives informing our prayers, giving them an urgency alongside the peace of God. We prayed for the world, which we were very much in, and for our parishioners, churchgoers or not. We prayed for those we knew and those we did not know. We lifted up that busy place to God, praying for God's peace for those who rushed off early in the morning to catch the train to London, returning late in the evening, only to do it all again the next day. We prayed for those who worried about their children or their elderly parents. And we prayed for those who were reaching the end of their lives. And then we sat in silence, exhausted at the thought of all that busyness and struggle. But it was our privilege to pray.

I will always be grateful to the Church of England for the full-time training it gave me – two years devoted to study and formation. They were not easy years, but they grounded me in prayer and taught me to work within its daily rhythm. There, I learnt to create services suitable for different occasions and to use them to encourage others, too, to pray.

Tealights were de rigueur as an aid. They filled floors and shelves, giving of themselves in services that we had devised in groups. We encouraged others to pray what was on their hearts, in the silence and out loud, all the while encompassed by the words we found in the official liturgy. We wrestled with silence – so hard, we thought, for many. Just how many minutes of silence could we expect a congregation to stand before they became uncomfortable – concerned, as when there is a tiny gap in a radio presentation and you worry that something has gone wrong? We learned to put together services for occasions of all kinds – to tailor them to the needs of the congregation we could expect to attend. How do you help a non-churchgoing family who have lost a dearly loved member to pray, when prayer is unfamiliar? We may have been learning to create prayers for our forthcoming parishioners, but that learning moved us forward in our own prayer lives.

Moving to a parish, one of the most joyful aspects was to work with the congregation as we learned to pray together. While training for ministry is stretching, it can send you down a path where your only companions – the ones who understand your spirituality – are clergy. It may even be a special path for priests who trained at your college with its own particular flavour. In a parish you are plunged once again into companionship with a huge variety of people, who may have no sense of needing to get it "right".

They bring their thoughts, experiences and approaches. They stretch you further, bringing the unexpected and the joy of a completely different point of view.

In an Easter article in *The Times*, the journalist Simon Barnes wrote about the Easter bunny, who, he pointed out, is in fact a hare. Far from the cute predictable rabbit, sitting by the edge of the road as you drive by, the hare suddenly springs out of nowhere. The small mound of grass turns out to be a living thing, which leaps in the air and bounds away unpredictably. The sheer breadth of the Anglican Communion ensures that, just when you felt comfortable with the rabbit, you are confronted by a hare, taking you off in some new and wild direction. You may explore the prayers of Walsingham, Iona, Taizé and much more, all within the framework that keeps you moving forward on the road. If you have no time to think, you can still pray, because someone has written some words for you. You can make them your own and, like the hare, they will surprise you with meaning when you least expect it. But Anglicans are not afraid to explore the prayers of other traditions and, if you have space for contemplation, resources and help are always at hand.

For many the goal of contemplation is silence. Mother Teresa, when asked about her prayer life, said that she didn't talk, but simply listened. Her interviewer asked what God said to her. "He also doesn't talk. He also simply listens," she replied.

The interviewer was understandably confused.

"If you can't understand the meaning of what I've just said, I'm sorry but there's no way I can explain it any better," she responded.

Thankfully there are many Anglicans who can lead you to a place where her words are true for you. Or, if you'd rather, to a different place, as God prompts.

If you are interested in meditation and contemplative prayer, the Book of Common Prayer may not be your first thought. Although it played its part in my growing understanding of prayer, its services were never my first preference, not least because attending a communion service usually involved getting up for eight o'clock! But it *is* a service of contemplation; ask anyone who regularly attends. For the band of eight o'clockers across the country, Sunday is not complete unless it has begun with BCP Holy Communion. The four-hundred-year-old language is an aid to calm and quiet meditation on God. It is pure joy. Perhaps there is a gap for spiritual directors who base their direction on its words, so precious and helpful to many.

My path of meditation began with the nuns, whom I continued to visit. A whole luxurious day spent in silence, punctuated by the Offices of the Sisters, with not a word spoken, left space that God could fill. Anglicans have taught me the Jesus Prayer, an ancient Eastern form of meditation sometimes prayed using a knotted cord, with a petition repeated at every knot, "Lord Jesus Christ, Son of God, have mercy on me, a sinner." They have gently shown me the way of Ignatian prayer. I have imagined myself in Bible stories, a bystander or character asking Jesus what he means by what he said, or what I am to understand by the events described.

I have explored praying with icons, as with the set in Winchester Cathedral, which stand behind the altar forming a deesis, or place of supplication. Nine gloriously gold and bright-coloured icons stand in a row – Christ is at the centre, the Virgin Mary is on his right and St John the Baptist on his left. Then come the two archangels, Michael and Gabriel, Saints Peter and Paul and the local saints, Birinus and Swithun. Colours and form are full of ancient meaning for those who know. But for those who don't, the icons still invite the one who looks to pray. You may believe you are there to ask at this place of supplication, and so you are, but "Let me lead you, and let me tell you more about yourself as I gaze on you from my place here," they seem to say.

It may seem odd to have moved from the words of the liturgy, which so inspired me, to silence and contemplation, but perhaps I can best explain by saying that my journey in prayer has led me to a place where I understand that those things which seem opposite are often exactly the same. Silence and recited words in prayer are different aspects of the same deep spirituality, just as God is the great presence and the great absence.

But I have not said, so far, that one of the greatest joys is not my own prayer, but the prayers of those who pray for me. The great Anglican community, taught to pray, has sustained me with prayer through the tough times. It continues to do so. I know there are those who watch, and think, and notice – and I hope to be part of that watchful community that prays unceasingly for all in need. In the convent chapel a nun is always at prayer, silently bringing the needs of the world and of the individual to God. I know that other, very different kinds of Anglicans, pray for me and for the world. And my own congregations support and pray for me, without judgement, but with love.

My journey is not ended, but I can see its shape. There is something precious about the place we start, and something infinitely valuable about the place that allows us to journey and the people who travel with us. From contemplation, every Sunday, we return to words. The liturgy once again conveys our prayers to God, together, with one voice.

I return to the beginning. T. S. Eliot understood that return, expressing its significance in his much-quoted poem:

> With the drawing of this Love and the voice of this Calling
> We shall not cease from exploration
> And the end of all our exploring
> Will be to arrive where we started
> And know the place for the first time.

> T. S. Eliot, "Little Gidding"

I will for ever be grateful to the Anglican Communion for all it has given me in prayer – for the journey on which it has taken me, and still takes me. It has its faults and its trials, and surely it ties itself in knots that seem impossible to release. But step back a little with me, kneel in your cathedral or at the altar of your parish church. Let the atmosphere, built up by centuries of prayer, or, if your church is new, by just a few years, penetrate deep into your soul. Rejoice with me that you are a part of it all. Move forward on your own journey of prayer, joyfully.

The Joy of Relationships for an Anglican

by Dr Muthuraj Swamy

Muthuraj is Associate Professor and Dean of the Faculty of Theology and Ethics at Union Biblical Seminary, Pune, North India, and General Editor of the Mission Theology in the Anglican Communion project. His book, *The Problem with Interreligious Dialogue: Plurality, Conflict and Elitism in Hindu-Christian-Muslim Relations*, was published by Bloomsbury in 2016.

To be Anglican is to be in relationship; it is to be in communion. The reality of relationship – both between God and human beings and among human beings – is essential for Anglican faith, identity and life. Without this, it is impossible to understand and interpret the Anglican way of Christian life. In this chapter I discuss how Anglicanism values relationships at various levels, and I reflect on the joy of relationships for an Anglican. I have chosen three areas in which Anglican relationships are vividly expressed. Firstly, in the Anglican Communion, which consists of millions of Christians, who may come from many diverse national, ethnic, linguistic, cultural, social, political and economic backgrounds, but who are united in a relationship that goes back for generations and hundreds of years. Next, I look at the ongoing efforts of Anglicans to engage in dialogue and create relationships with various Christian denominations. Finally, I discuss how Anglicans build relationships with other religions and cultures in order to maintain a close connection between Church and society.

The contemporary social and ecclesial context: the need for building relationships

One of the fundamental questions asked by Christianity is: "What is my relationship with God and my neighbour?" Religions in general are occupied with the question: "Who am I?" but the question: "What am I in relation to God and my neighbour?" is central for Christianity. Jesus succinctly expresses this through his answer to the question on the greatest commandment in Matthew 22:35-40. This is basically a question about relationships. The triangular relationship between "you, your God and your neighbour" makes Christianity a religion of relationships, and has made the Church what it is. Christianity emphasises the relationships between people, or more specifically, the followers of Jesus Christ, as the central or core tenet of religion. Most importantly, Christianity envisions that social relationships are centred on divine intervention in the world, and this is why we are able to speak about a doctrine like the Trinity in terms of relationships between human beings.

Thus the very existence of Christianity is based on the understanding of relationships and the task of building or promoting them, and the life and teachings of Jesus Christ remain foundational for the Church in continuing to carry this out. This simply means that the Church should just live out what it is. In other words, the Church itself is a web of relationships, and in that context building Church and building relationships are not two different things but are simply the same. Therefore we do not need to speak of Church and relationship, or relationship in the Church, but simply Church *as* relationship, or Church as communion, or *koinonia*.[1]

However, in spite of the presence of Christianity/Church for more than two millennia, we see today that relationships are deteriorating at many levels. The world is said to be progressing in scientific, technological, educational and economic advancements, but we also witness a growing number of relationship problems on all levels – from the breakdown of family relationships, to gangs, sectarianism and wars between nations. And of course relationship problems also often affect the Church. Building relationships within the Church – among the laity, between various groups within the Church, between clergy and laity, and between those who minister and those to whom they minister – has become an urgent need today. Also, the borders between various Churches and denominations have to be crossed to build relationships. One of the inevitable consequences of the Protestant Reformation is the growth in the number of denominations, but in the twenty-first century we also are becoming aware of the need for better relationships and cooperation between different Churches. In addition, the borders between the Church and various aspects of society, especially other religions, is also a test for the very meaning and existence of the Church. In all these three areas the Church has to cross borders in order to build relationships.

In such a context, the joy for an Anglican is that the Anglican Communion has seriously attempted to build relationships in these three areas, in spite of all the shortcomings in these processes. Along with the joy, however, comes responsibility, as we shall see.

Building and maintaining relationships within the Anglican Communion

One of the most prominent ways through which Anglican commitment to relationships is expressed is through building and maintaining relationships between different Churches within the worldwide Anglican Communion. Even though the visible nature of the Anglican Communion as an organisation emerged as a result of the First Lambeth Conference in 1867, relationships between the various Churches within the Anglican Communion go back centuries. True, the Church of England, which is seen as the mother Church, exists within English national boundaries and under British jurisdiction. However, Anglicanism is built not strictly on national

---

1 *Koinonia* is the Greek word for communion.

boundaries, but rather on relationships that go beyond these limitations, even though the term "Anglican" may itself have geographical connotations. Thus to be Anglican is to be in a relationship that crosses many borders and boundaries.

The feature essential for building and maintaining these relationships lies in celebrating difference and diversity rather than looking for uniformity or homogeneity. In world history, as well as ecclesial history, there is ample evidence to show that the push for uniformity rather than celebrating difference and diversity is detrimental to relationships. As we shall see, Anglicanism has very clearly, strongly and consciously attempted to overcome such temptations.

From time to time, efforts have been made to create a central authority or system in the Anglican Communion, especially in times of crisis. But the Anglican Communion as a whole does not have an authoritative statement of its identity or beliefs. Hence one of the most important problems in Anglicanism continues to be the search for a centralised authority.[2] Sometimes attempts have been made to overcome this problem by seeing Anglican authority as rooted in the ancient or Reformation tradition, and sometimes by attempting to establish a common system that can manage all the Churches in the Anglican Communion. An attempt, perhaps, to create something along the lines of an Anglican Pope!

For instance, immediately after the First Lambeth Conference Bishop George Selwyn, Bishop of Lichfield (1809-1878), strongly pushed to create a centralised Anglican authority for the Anglican Communion, and those who supported this idea brought it to the Second Lambeth Conference. However this attempt did not succeed. Mark Chapman, a prominent author on Anglicanism, says that the Lambeth Conference recommended that "the duly certified action of every national or particular Church... in the exercise of its own discipline, should be respected by all the other Churches, and by their individual members". There was to be no meddling in the affairs of other Churches and no central tribunal, and it was decided that, "Every ecclesiastical province... should be held responsible for its own decisions in the exercise of... discipline."[3] Chapman comments that whenever a push for a centralised authority became strong, nevertheless "diversity and elasticity won out against centralism and uniformity."[4]

---

2 Mark Chapman, *Anglicanism: A Very Short Introduction* (Oxford: University Press, 2006), 4.
3 Chapman, *Anglicanism*, 117.
4 Chapman, *Anglicanism*, 117-118.

Similarly, the 1948 Lambeth Conference report says:

> Authority, as inherited by the Anglican Communion from the
> undivided Church of the early centuries of the Christian era,
> is single in that it is derived from a single Divine source, and
> reflects within itself the richness and historicity of the divine
> Revelation… It is distributed among Scripture, Tradition,
> Creeds, the Ministry of the Word and Sacraments, the witness
> of saints, and the consensus fidelium, which is the continuing
> experience of the Holy Spirit through His faithful people in the
> Church. It is thus a dispersed rather than a centralized authority
> having many elements which combine, interact with, and check
> each other… [5]

What is particularly interesting is that what remains a centralised authority
for Anglicanism is the multifarious relationships and interactions that are
found within the Communion. In reality, the Communion is held together
by a shared history. This in some circles is known as a peculiar experience
of authority. What is meant here is that authority is replaced by the belief
in mutual relationship. One Anglican scholar and priest, Callan Slipper,
expresses it thus:

> The Anglican advantage… is rooted in a peculiar experience of
> authority. The community experience of discernment… requires
> everyone to play his or her part. This means that the learned and
> those with a particular experience, mystical or otherwise, and
> even those who speak out of their grasp of life but have no special
> claim to knowledge, all have a responsibility along with those
> who have a personal charism for discernment as one aspect of
> their position of leadership. This gives rise to what has been called
> "dispersed authority".[6]

Even though some within the Anglican Communion have attempted
to create a centralised authority, the real ground of authority for an
Anglican is found nowhere other than in the very relationship that has
been built between various Churches. Favouring mutual relationships
over central authority has been the fundamental thing that has held the
Communion together.

5 *The Lambeth Conference* (London, 1948) Report IV. "The Anglican Communion", 84, cited in Callan Slipper, "Why I Am an
   Anglican and Believe I Shall Remain So". www.stbonifacetrust.org.uk/documents/slipper-callan.pdf, accessed 30 May 2017.
6 Slipper, "Why I Am an Anglican and Believe I Shall Remain So". www.stbonifacetrust.org.uk/documents/slipper-
   callan.pdf.

In spite of official statements regarding the diversity of the Anglican Communion, some contemporary theologians still hold that there is an identity crisis in Anglicanism and it is due to the lack of a common system. Interpreting identity as communion, the theologian Chul-Lai Ro argues that:

> Anglican identity is bound up in the question of how Anglicans live in the life of communion. This means that our questions about Anglican identity cannot be answered without incorporating them within the idea of communion. In other words, there can be no Anglican identity without communion with one another, with the world, and with God.[7]

This was vividly expressed in the "Report of the Pastoral and Dogmatic Concerns" of the 1988 Lambeth Conference: "The fundamental theological question about the identity of Anglicanism is what it means for a Christian to be in communion."[8]

In addition, the Anglican Communion is held together by liturgy and prayer, which offer Anglicans a way of relating to God and one another. In the context of Roman Catholic theology's veneration of the consecrated elements of the Eucharist, Thomas Cranmer interpreted Holy Communion as spiritual nourishment for the life of Christians. Slipper says:

> No wonder what the Articles call "the supper of the Lord" was titled in the Book of Common Prayer as The Lord's Supper or Holy Communion and subsequently generally referred to only as The Communion. The emphasis is upon the transformative encounter with Jesus. We come to know him and enter into a new, profound relationship with him, one that fulfils the work begun in our liturgical hearing of the Word, hence the Sacrament brings about our Christification at every level of our being... [9]

My own experience is that Anglican worship and liturgy offer enormous resources, not only for relating with God in prayer and fellowship, but for building relationships with fellow members in the Church. As a convert to Christianity at the tender age of seven, it was these relationships that I witnessed in the lives of worshipping Christians during and after Sunday worship, that made me respond positively to my pastor's invitation to attend church regularly and join the Sunday school.

---

7 Chul-Lai Ro, "Towards the Renewal of Anglican Identity as Communion: The Relationship of the Trinity, *Missio Dei*, and Anglican Comprehensiveness." PhD thesis submitted to Cardiff University, (2008), 90.
8 Cited in Ro, "Towards the Renewal of Anglican Identity as Communion", 90.
9 Slipper, "Why I Am an Anglican and Believe I Shall remain So".

Anglican efforts for ecumenical relationships

Another area where the Anglican commitment to relationships can be found is in ecumenism. More than ever today there is urgency in various denominations and Churches to work together on concerns that affect society in many parts of the world – poverty, violence, social and ethnic exclusion, political instability, corruption and economic exploitation, to name but a few. For over a hundred years, ecumenism has grown significantly, and the Anglican Communion has played a central role. The Lambeth Conference of 1920 expressed a strong commitment to the visible unity of all Christians. This opened up ways of initiating ecumenical discussions with Orthodox Churches and the European Catholic Churches which had separated from Rome. Representatives from these Churches were invited to send observers to the 1930 Lambeth Conference. Relations with the Church of Sweden also became fruitful and by 1993, when the Porvoo Agreement was drawn up, intercommunion with most of the Nordic and British Churches had become a reality.[10]

These ecumenical relations within the Anglican Communion encouraged the negotiations in South India that began in the first decade of the twentieth century. In this union four denominations – Anglican, Presbyterian, Congregationalist and Methodist – came together to establish the Church of South India in 1947, the year India attained independence from British colonial rule. These ecumenical efforts influenced the formation of the Church of North India in 1970 and also the Church of Pakistan. As a member of the Church of South India, I am always aware of the importance of these ecumenical relationships, which need to be taken still further.

The ecumenical spirit has been nurtured by various archbishops of Canterbury and in the Lambeth Conferences that they convened. Michael Ramsey, Archbishop of Canterbury during the 1960s, argued that Anglican theology was not "confessionalism". According to him, all Churches point beyond themselves to:

> … the Gospel of God by which alone, in which alone, in one universal family, mankind can be made perfect. It is not something Roman or Greek or Anglican; rather does it declare to men their utter dependence upon Christ by setting forth the universal Church in which all that is Anglican or Roman or Greek or partial or local in any way must share in an agonizing death to its pride.[11]

---

10 Chapman, *Anglicanism*, 129.
11 Chapman, *Anglicanism*, 131.

What really matters is that the ecumenical relations of the Anglican Communion are essential for its self-reflection. In other words, commitment to ecumenism is not simply one of the tasks of the Anglican Communion, but in being a communion its very being is built on ecumenism. Thus the many ecumenical dialogues in which the Anglican Communion has participated provide old ground for being a communion in and of themselves. In other words, "Anglicanism has come to understand more about itself and its theology of 'Communion' through its ecumenical discussions with other churches." This is a crucial point, because it is the word "Communion" which holds Anglicanism together.[12]

Faithful to their identity and vision of the Communion, Anglican Churches worldwide today are involved in ecumenical relations with many other denominations. Anglican-Baptist, Anglican-Reformed, Anglican-Orthodox and Anglican-Catholic dialogue and relations are some examples of the Anglican Communion's continued commitment to ecumenical relations. What a joy it is to be part of a Communion which continues to strive to build relationships with other Churches!

Anglican initiatives for interfaith dialogue and relations

In addition to having strong ties with other Churches, Anglicanism is also deeply committed to building and maintaining relationships with people of other religions. In fact, in a world where factors such as globalisation and migration are bringing multiculturalism into sharp focus, developing and nurturing interreligious relations is becoming an urgent imperative.

The Anglican commitment to interreligious relations is in fact founded on the Anglican vision of society. Anglican historical tradition holds Church and society together, rather than as binaries or polarised structures of human life. As one Anglican theologian, Wendy Dackson, notes:

> For Anglican Christians, Church and society can never be separated; they are integral to each other. Society, whether civil or ecclesial, is where persons are shaped and characters formed. Any foretaste of the kingdom is grounded in the social life of the world. Furthermore, society is not only the locus of salvation; it is also the object of salvation.[13]

---

12 Peter Foley, "Anglican Communion: A Theological Consideration". www.msgr.ca/msgr-3/Anglican%20Communion%20a%20Theological%20Consideration.pdf, accessed 28 May 2017.
13 Wendy Dackson, "Anglicanism and Social Theology" in *Anglican Theological Review*, 94:4 (Fall 2012), 616.

Among many theologians in the Anglican tradition, Richard Hooker is perhaps the strongest voice for this approach. In his most famous work, *The Laws of Ecclesiastical Polity*, he argued that Church and society were essentially identical.[14] As the Anglican tradition has Church-society integration at its core, relating with other religions has occupied a significant place in the Anglican Communion.

Many Anglican missionaries who were sent to places where they met people of other major or indigenous religions, especially in Asia and Africa, were committed to building and maintaining relationships with other religions. John William Colenso (1814-1883), the first Bishop of Natal, is one such example. Rather than insisting that indigenous African people be converted wholesale to Anglican Christianity, Colenso caused outrage by arguing that the traditional African practice of polygamy ought to be tolerated, and refused to preach that the ancestors of converted Africans were condemned to damnation.

Attempts on the part of Anglicans to build relationships with people from other faiths continue to this day. Following the attack on the World Trade Center in September 2001, the Anglican Communion has, in a number of ways and at a number of levels, striven to build relationships with Islamic leaders, organisations and grass-roots Muslims. The former Archbishop of Canterbury, Rowan Williams, was directly involved in some of these networks, particularly in the Building Bridges project, which organises annual seminars for Christian and Muslim scholars.

Reflecting on one seminar, he wrote:

> … at the end of that seminar, at which we had discussed the nature and the place of scripture within our faiths, I commented that I had been encouraged by the quality of our disagreement. Inevitably, tackling so central a theological issue, we had frequently come up against points on which we differed; however, we had done so in ways that did not undermine our relationships but rather kept us open to learning from each other.[15]

---

14 Richard Hooker, in Arthur Stephen McGrade (ed.), *The Laws of Ecclesiastical Polity*, Book VIII (Cambridge: University Press, 1989), 1.2.

15 Rowan Williams, "Foreword", in David D. Grafton, Joseph F. Duggan and Jason Craige Harris (eds), *Christian-Muslim Relations in the Anglican and Lutheran Communions* (New York: Palgrave Macmillan, 2013), xiii. The Society of Anglican and Lutheran Theologians (SALT) has brought out this volume, which is a good resource for Christian-Muslim relations.

Another initiative was the Christian-Muslim Forum, which was launched in 2006. Its objectives were:

> ... to engage Muslims and Christians at the grassroots level over practical issues of shared concern, including both potential problems for our relationships and also opportunities for positive Muslim-Christian cooperation and contribution to the common good.[16]

The Network for Interfaith Concerns (NIFCON) in the Anglican Communion has been very active in the last few years and is contributing to Anglican initiatives in various interfaith forums.[17] The dialogue between the Anglican Communion and Al-Azhar Al-Sharif, the Islamic institution in Cairo, which was launched in 2002, is another significant interfaith relationship. Mission Theology in the Anglican Communion (MTAC) is another ongoing project that works for dialogue and relationships between theologians of global north and south, with a focus on sharing knowledge about interreligious dialogue and efforts for reconciliation between communities.[18]

Not only the Anglican Communion based in the UK, but also different Anglican Churches in Africa and Asia are continuing their work in building relationships with other religions. Many Church of South India and Church of North India theologians have engaged in interreligious dialogue with people of other religions, especially Hindus in India. Similarly local Christian churches in countries like Nigeria are involved in various initiatives with Muslim groups. In the USA the Episcopal Church's Office of Ecumenical and Interfaith Relations develops, nurtures and promotes relations with people from all religions.

In recent years, concerns about migration and the refugee crisis have also led Anglicans to become directly involved in building relationships with refugees who are mostly Muslims. The present Archbishop of Canterbury Justin Welby's efforts, and the Anglican Communion's initiatives to welcome refugees from all religions, clearly shows how important many Anglicans consider it to be.

---

16 Williams, "Foreword", xii.
17 http://nifcon.anglicancommunion.org, accessed 31 May 2017.
18 http://www.missiontheologyanglican.org, accessed 31 May 2017.

Conclusion

Thus my joy in being Anglican emerges from the Anglican commitment to relationships – relationships within the Anglican Communion itself, relationships with other Churches and denominations, and relationships with people of other faiths. What I have discussed and reflected can convey only a small part of what the Anglican Communion does with regard to this, but provides my personal observation and reflection about how relationships remain fundamental to Anglicanism. I have selected only a few examples to illustrate my point.

Let me conclude with the words of Mark Chapman, who discusses different possibilities for keeping the Anglican Communion together. One of the possibilities is this:

> … diversity and comprehensiveness might be at the heart of an Anglicanism that understands itself more as a way of muddling through to the truth than a set of definitive judgements. The desire to listen and to enter into conversation requires voluntary restraint and self-denial among the different factions. The problem is that in a world which seeks clear decisions and absolute certainties such Christian humility might not any longer be considered a virtue.[19]

My own thinking is that, after all, when humility was considered a vice in the Hellenistic (Greek) context in which Christianity arose,[20] Jesus Christ and his followers could re-establish it as a virtue and establish Christianity, not basically as religion, but as a relationship with God and one's neighbours. Similarly, in spite of the identity crises and push for a centralised authority in a communion consisting of diverse groups of people, Anglicanism did nurture Christian humility built on relationships and respect for diversity and difference. My hope and joy is that it will continue to do so in years to come.

---

19 Chapman, *Anglicanism*, 143-144.
20 Early Christianity was heavily influenced by Greek culture and ideas. Thus, you could, for shorthand, say that Christianity is an amalgamation of Hebrew and Greek ideas – and, until relatively recently, Greek culture held sway. It is only since the middle of the twentieth century that Christians have paid more attention to the Hebrew roots of their faith, leading to, for example, attempts to understand Christianity in terms of soul and body (Hebrew), where soul had previously been emphasised. Some of Jesus' teachings (such as humility) were diametrically opposed to both Hebrew and Greek culture.

The Joy of Education for an Anglican Woman

by the Revd Dr Lydia Mwaniki

Lydia is the Director of Theology, Family Life and Gender Justice in the All-Africa Conference of Churches (AACC), and the African Editor of the Mission Theology in the Worldwide Anglican Communion project. Before joining the AACC she was a lecturer at St Paul's University, Kenya, where she also acted as the Dean of Students. She is a board member of the Ecumenical Disability Advocacy Network (EDAN), a World Council of Churches programme, a member of the African Council for Accreditation and Accountability (AFCAA), and an elected member of the Standing Committee of Synod in Nairobi.

Education is a fundamental right to which every human being is entitled. Not only that, but it is key to the sustainable development and success of every nation. The importance of education is underscored by the United Nations in its Sustainable Development Goal (SDG) 4, to "Ensure inclusive and equitable quality education and promote lifelong learning opportunities for all."[1]

Women's education is crucial for the development of a nation, since women constitute over half of the world's population and bring their unique talents to education, with national, community, family and individual benefits. Although education has given women a lot of joy and privilege, however, unfortunately many have experienced disparities in education in many parts of the world, especially because of cultural, religious, legal and policy factors that create inequity and inequality in education.

In this chapter I will tell the story of my own education an Anglican woman born and raised in Kenya. I will also look at women's education in Kenya, from its introduction by missionaries, with particular focus on the role of the Church Mission Society (CMS) and independent Kenya in promoting women's formal education.

The joy of education for an Anglican woman

I was born and brought up in the Anglican Church of Kenya (ACK) as part of a third generation of Christians. My maternal grandparents, Lydia and Ishmael Nduki, were among the first Christians when CMS established a mission station in Kabare, Central Kenya in 1910, where my grandfather became an evangelist and was very involved with his local Kiamiciri Anglican-sponsored primary school.

My parents, Agnes and Peter Ndambiri Muciri, tell me that the first people to see me and pray for me immediately after my birth were CMS missionaries. When my mother was in labour, my father went to the mission station and requested that the missionaries drive my mother to hospital, since there was no other available transport in the neighbourhood. However, on arrival at my parents' homestead, the missionaries found that I had just been born with the help of a traditional midwife, so they prayed for me.

One of the marks of a committed Christian was that, besides attending church, his or her children had to go to school. Coming from a Christian

1 United Nations, Sustainable Development Knowledge Platform. https://sustainabledevelopment.un.org/sdg4, accessed 30 May 2017.

background therefore paved the way for me to go to school at the age of six. However, girls' education was still viewed with contempt by some people in the community. My parents therefore suffered ridicule from their neighbours, not only for giving birth to five girls and only one boy (born last), but also for educating the girls.

After completing my primary education in a government primary school, in 1980 I went to Karoti Girls' Secondary School, an Anglican-sponsored school in Central Kenya and in 1984 I started to attend Matuga Girls' High school. It was in these schools that my Christian faith was nurtured and deepened through active participation and leadership in the Christian Union (CU).

After completing high school in 1985, I felt a strong call to offer myself fully to the service of God. In 1987 I was admitted to St Andrew's College of Theology and Development, an Anglican institution founded by CMS missionaries as a mission station. I pursued a three-year certificate in theology between 1987 and 1989. While I was there, I got an opportunity to go to St John's College, Nottingham on an exchange programme, not only on account of my academic performance, but also because I was the Vice Senior Student. I was the first student in our college to do so.

After I completed my certificate in theology, my female classmates and I were made lay readers and then commissioned as deaconesses, while our male classmates were made deacons and then ordained to priesthood after a one-year probation. Ordination of women to priesthood in the Diocese of Kirinyaga came only later, in 1992, after long, heated debates in a series of diocesan synods.[2]

I was married to Daniel Stakos Mwaniki, an Anglican priest, in December 1989. In 1992 I joined St Paul's University, Kenya, where I was sponsored by my diocese, ACK Diocese of Embu. I was a young mother and my firstborn son, Johnmoses, was only two years old, and I was expecting my second child, Ann, to whom I gave birth in my first year. In the second year I gave birth to my youngest child, Peter. It was a huge challenge bringing up three babies and being a student at the same time. Besides, we had very little income, since as a student I was entitled to an allowance of only $18 a month.

With the help of my husband, who was earning $25 a month, we managed to take care of the family. I also passed with a good degree.

2 Lydia M. Mwaniki, "The Impact of the Church on the Development of the Identity of an African Christian Woman: A Case Study of the Anglican Church of Kenya, Diocese of Kirinyaga 1910-1999-2000". Master's dissertation (Pietermaritzburg: University of Natal, 2000), 64-65.

My graduation opened an opportunity for me to teach at St Andrew's, Kabare in 1995 where I got a scholarship from the African Theological Fellowship to pursue a Masters of Theology in African Christianity (MTH) at the University of Kwazulu Natal, South Africa, and later a PhD in theology, specialising in New Testament and gender. I was sponsored by the Langham Partnership[3] and the World Council of Churches (WCC). I graduated in 2011. Sadly, however, I was a widow by this time, as my husband had died in August 2004.

After graduating with my PhD and receiving an award for academic excellence from the university chancellor, I was employed as a lecturer at St Paul's University, Kenya, where I taught New Testament and gender studies until 2015.

For me personally, education has empowered me to venture into a domain which is traditionally reserved for men. It has debunked the idea that women cannot be leaders in the Church and society. It has opened opportunities for me to travel in Africa, the USA and Europe. It has enabled me to engage with church leaders, other religious leaders and scholars. I have been published online and in books and journals. I will for ever be grateful to the various individuals and organisations which have empowered me and other women by promoting gender equality in education.

The Church Mission Society (CMS) and the beginnings of formal education in Kenya

The history of CMS in Kenya goes back to 1844, when Dr Johann Ludwig Krapf, a CMS missionary, started mission work at the Kenyan coast. By 1910, the CMS had moved up country and planted churches in the central part of Kenya (Kikuyuland), following the British colonial occupation of the area. Missionaries introduced Western education to Kenya with the establishment of the first mission school in 1846 at Rabai, near Mombasa. The education system was set up by the colonial government in the country in 1926. Besides promoting European interests, education was officially a means of spreading Christianity. Schools served as centres for teaching catechism. The missionaries set up mission schools, particularly in the central and western parts of Kenya, which were suitable for European settlement, while avoiding those regions, especially among the pastoral tribes, which were thought to be either lawless or economically unviable.

---

3 A global fellowship founded by John Stott, an evangelical Anglican minister. The name Langham comes from All Souls' Church, Langham Place, London. See http://uk.langham.org.

The local people received education with mixed reactions. While some embraced it, others rejected it, especially because of its link to colonisation. Some locals also perceived the education of their children as a gain for the missionaries, and therefore expected compensation. For instance, the people of Sagala, who were disappointed by the inability of the missionaries to meet their economic expectations, told J. Wray, the founder of the initially unsuccessful Taita station: "White man, you are living in our country, but you don't buy our ivory, cattle or slaves; neither do you pay our children for coming to school. We feel we are not getting the profit out of you we had hoped for."[4]

The European system of education also had racial and gender inequalities, which led to the introduction of African schools and churches. Firstly, there was a racial bias in enrolment in both primary and secondary schools. According to a survey in 1962, Africans came lowest, with just 4.7 per cent enrolled in education, followed by Arabs (36.9) and Asians (77.5). Europeans were top on the list with 84.6 per cent. Also, since education was very politicised, the curriculum for Kenyans initially prepared only men to advance in colonial politics and economic interests. Africans reacted strongly against this biased curriculum, which was later revised by the missionaries, and opportunities were opened for further education abroad.

According to Tabitha Kanogo, up until the early 1950s, the missionaries were not keen to impart academic skills to women. Instead, girls were prepared to be homemakers. A CMS mission conference held in 1942 on "Women's and Girls' Work", for instance, recommended that; "Education should have as its goal the training of girls themselves for home-making… girls' teachers are best employed in teaching in the kindergarten and in teaching girls' subjects throughout the rest of the school."[5] Nevertheless, in early 1950 the government changed the education policy for girls in secondary schools. The missionaries reviewed their strategies periodically to accommodate girls who wished to pursue careers.[6]

In 1966, at a women's seminar, a number of challenges were presented as obstacles to women's education. Some of them still persist today in Kenya:[7]

- The fear that higher education for girls minimised their chances of getting married.

---

4 R. W. Strayer, *The Making of Mission Communities in East Africa* (London: Heinmann, 1978), 65.
5 Kenya National Archives (KNA Mss/61/567) "Women and Girls' Education 1943".
6 Tabitha Kanogo, "Mission Impact on Women in Colonial Kenya", in F. Bowie, D. Kirkwood and S. Ardener (eds), *Women and Missions: Past and Present Anthropological and Historical Perceptions* (Oxford: Berg, 1993), 165-186.
7 Mwaniki, "The impact of the Church on the Development of the Identity of an African Christian Woman".

- A strong cultural belief in the local community that girls would eventually get married and education was not required for marriage. Some parents also felt that they were educating a wife for another man.

- Early marriages and unplanned pregnancies for school-age girls leading to dropping out of school.

- The suspicion that formal schools did not instil discipline. Therefore some communities like the Maasai opted to continue with their traditional education for girls.

- Parental preference for sons' education over that of daughters, because girls would be married off anyway, but boys would provide security for their ageing parents.

- The gender division of labour, whereby girls spent more time after school helping their mothers with household chores, which was not traditionally required from boys.

Despite its shortcomings and challenges, however, the contribution of Christian missions to education can by no means be underestimated. Preparing women to be homemakers, although creating gender disparity, equipped them to be instruments of transformation in the fields of agriculture, health, hygiene and education.

While the common representation of African women was that they were "dependent social victims",[8] this was countered by the missionary training which enabled women to become financially independent. Women who gained employment in teaching and nursing, or who became domestic workers in European houses, or who sewed clothes for sale, were no longer dependent on their parents financially. This of course allowed them some independence from the control of their parents and other social constraints, especially where they worked away from home.[9] Further, as Kanogo observes, missionary education opened leadership opportunities for women, particularly in the Church, as leaders of women's organisations such as the Mothers' Union and the Women's Guild.[10]

---

8 Tabitha Kanogo, *African Womanhood in Colonial Kenya: 1900-50* (Oxford: James Carey, 2005), 9.
9 The Chief Native Commissioner (CNC) John Ainsworth, who was perturbed by the indigenous power structures that denied women freedom to work outside their homes, wrote to the Solicitor General in April 1919, enquiring about the possibility of legislation that would allow native women to attain majority status at the age of twenty-one. He hoped that such legislation would enable women to work anywhere they wished away from home (see Kanogo, 2005, 19).
10 Tabitha Kanogo, "Mission Impact on Women in Colonial Kenya", 165-186.

The CMS missionaries found some of the Kikuyu cultural practices oppressive to women and an obstacle to their education. These included the dowry, female circumcision, polygamy and the custom of levirate marriage, whereby the brother of a deceased man is obliged to marry his late brother's widow. They therefore made every effort to condemn these practices, even in the face of great opposition and resistance from the pre-colonial Kenyan communities and authorities.

The government's role in education

Soon after independence in December 1963, the Ominde Commission was established to inform the government about the existing educational resources, as well as to give advice on the formulation and implementation of national policies for education. Anglican-sponsored schools were continued after independence and are still in existence, conforming to the government education system. Both boys and girls studied under a similar curriculum, although the rate of enrolment for girls in school continued to be lower than for boys. A detailed report of the government of Kenya's involvement with education for both boys and girls in primary, secondary and tertiary levels was produced in 2006.[11]

As a result of the numerous factors that disadvantage women in education, Kenya has made various strides to bridge the gap. The introduction of free primary education (FPE) in Kenya in 2003, for example, not only improved the rate of enrolment for both boys and girls, but also enabled more girls, who would previously be denied education in favour of their brothers, to go to school. Promulgation of the new constitution in Kenya was the greatest stride towards gender equity and equality, since its laws are geared towards eradicating gender disparities.

In recognising the importance of women's education, Kenya launched a gender policy in education in 2016. The policy was aimed at creating gender equity and equality in education, particularly by addressing legal and policy concerns that perpetuated inequality between women and girls and men and boys. It was noted that the gender gap in favour of males widens as one goes higher up the education ladder. Indeed in some parts of the country today, such as Central Kenya, primary-school enrolment of girls is actually higher. Other initiatives, such as Kenya Vision 2030,[12] also promote gender equality, without which economic achievement would be difficult to realise.

---

11 Fatuma Chege and Eric Sifuna, "Girls' and Women's Education in Kenya: Gender Perspectives and Trends" (2006). www.researchgate.net/publication/44839870, accessed 16 May 2017.
12 www.vision2030.go.ke

Challenges for girls' education in Kenya today

Some of the obstacles to women's education in the missionary era continue as major hindrances in present-day Kenya:

- The widening of gender gaps in higher education in favour of men, among other factors, has resulted in fewer women having the ability to hold high positions of leadership and decision-making, participate fully in the political arena, and have access to and control of resources, among other disadvantages.

- Unpaid care work, whereby African women still, for example, carry out 71 per cent of water collecting, translating to forty billion hours a year.[13] This and a lot more unpaid care work limits the time women can spend in education and paid work.

- Gender-based violence is reported in some schools, where school-going girls have been reported as being abused sexually by their teachers, leading to unplanned pregnancies affecting their education.

- Harmful, retrogressive and fatal cultural beliefs and practices, such as under-age marriage and female genital mutilation (FGM) are experienced in some communities.

- Cultural beliefs that tough subjects such as science and technical subjects can only be pursued by boys in higher education. As a result, more girls are concentrated in the faculty of humanities, limiting their potential to compete for better jobs.

Nevertheless, besides these challenges, education has benefited women in many ways, as my own story shows.

Basic education has enabled women to become literate, opening opportunities for some to engage in decision-making processes, advance in business activities, assume positions of leadership, venture into the political arena and acquire confidence for self-expression to lobby support from the government, NGOs and other agencies, as well as being vocal about their rights. Education has equipped women with skills in vocations such as sewing, tailoring, knitting, embroidery, food processing and preparation, book-keeping and accounting, and has increased women's participation in the labour market and other fields. All these engagements are important

---

13 "The Africa Energy Outlook" (World Energy Outlook, 2014). www.iea.org/publications/freepublications/publication/ WEO2014_AfricaEnergyOutlook.pdf, accessed 31 May 2017.

for women's economic empowerment, and means of achieving the United Nations' Sustainable Development Goal (SDG) 1, which seeks to eradicate poverty by 2030. Other benefits of women's education are that education has reduced infant and maternal mortality rates, improved family health, improved agricultural activity and enabled women to take their children to school, since educated women are more likely to do so.[14]

Education has been instrumental in opening doors for women into professions that are traditionally associated with men, and has increased economic activity in Kenya. Nevertheless, education has not completely enabled the Church and society to challenge the traditional view that women are inferior. Men are still largely the preferred leaders in the public and political arena, and even in the Church. My recent research on gender representation in the organisational structure of the ACK between 2003 and 2013,[15] for example, reveals that women are highly underrepresented in all the three houses – the House of Bishops, the House of Clergy and the House of the Laity. In the ACK diocese of Nairobi, where I serve as a priest, ordained women constitute only 15.6 per cent of all ordained priests, while men constitute 84.4 per cent.[16] Besides, there is no woman bishop in the ACK, and only one in the Anglican Church in Africa.

As we can see, although there have been many positive steps, education has not yet fully empowered women to participate equally with men in top leadership positions in the ACK and in society at large. Cultural prejudices which relegate women to a subservient status have been reinforced by selective reading of some biblical texts, for example,[17] which are seen to subordinate women to men. There is work still to do. The Church, which is mandated by Jesus Christ to be the salt of the earth and the light of the world, needs to work with the government to remove barriers that hinder women from enjoying equal privileges and opportunities, so that they can experience the joy of education in its fullness, equally with men.

---

14 Ann Syomwene and Jonah Nyaga, "Women's Education and Economic Development in Kenya: Implications for Curriculum Development and Implementation Processes." *Journal of Education and Practice*, 6:15 (2015). www.iiste.org.
15 Lydia M. Mwaniki, "Women, Reconciliation and Mission: A Biblical Mandate". Paper presented during a webiner meeting, 26-30 March 2017.
16 ACK Diocese of Nairobi Establishment, September 2016.
17 Some of these include 1 Corinthians 11:1-16; 14:34-35; 1 Timothy 2:11-12 and Ephesians 5:22-24.

The Joy of Church Music for an Anglican

by Leigh Nixon

A chorister at Westminster Abbey in the early 1960s, Leigh subsequently won a choral scholarship at King's College Cambridge, where he read music. After a further two years' study in London, he began working with most of the London professional choirs and consorts, rapidly making a name for himself in the fields of early and contemporary music. Between 1985 and 2013 he returned to Westminster Abbey as a lay vicar, singing at many royal and state occasions. His other musical interests include work as an organist, choral director and singing teacher.

In this chapter Leigh is interviewed by Heather Smith.

Heather: I know you have a strong family connection with Westminster Abbey. Can you begin by telling me a little about it?

Leigh: My family connections go back to 1908. My paternal grandfather was a minor canon and later Precentor from 1912 until about 1933, when he retired to Lincolnshire. He could, apparently, just pick up an instrument and play it or sing. My own father was born at the abbey in 1909 and lived there most of his early life, except when at school or at Oxford. That grandfather died before I was born, but my granny had taught the violin and played the piano, and it was she who was my earliest musical influence and encouraged me to become a chorister.

My father worked at the British Museum and, when he retired in 1974 aged sixty-five, the abbey was looking for a librarian. My grandfather had acted as librarian (they did not have a full-time librarian at the time) and my father had done his apprenticeship there, so he returned.

Heather: Your own involvement began as a chorister. Tell me something about that.

Leigh: I joined a church choir in Dorking where I lived. Then, at the quite elderly age of ten I went to be a chorister at the abbey – in those days one left at fourteen; nowadays they tend to leave at about thirteen. The most exciting musician there at that time was the sub-organist Simon Preston, later to become organist and Master of the Choristers. As choristers we all absolutely adored him for his incredible verve and energy. He had recently been an organ scholar at King's College Cambridge under David Willcocks. David was still there when I went up as a choral scholar in 1970 and was perhaps the most profound influence on my professional life.

As a child I just tended to accept being at the abbey. It was quite a surprise to find out later, when going to another school, that other people had different experiences. We were up at seven in the morning. We did a run twice around Dean's Yard, had breakfast and went to the morning boys' practice which would last about an hour. Then we had a full day's schooling and at four o'clock we went over to the abbey for half an hour with the organist. The men in the choir joined us at half past four for a full choir rehearsal before Evensong at five.

I loved being there. There was no question at all. It was a musical training you couldn't beat. I learnt how to sight read without actually being aware of it, because you had to sing something like eight or nine services a week in term time. You learnt from your peers: as a junior you were placed beside a senior who would make sure you were on the right page! At the time there were twenty-two boys who sang daily, with an extra fourteen probationers waiting to come up into the choir proper. So the school itself had only the thirty-six pupils – tiny.

Heather: What did you sing as a chorister?

Leigh: When I joined in 1962 virtually everything we sang was in English. I don't think we even sang Latin anthems. If we did, Latin was a rarity. You didn't even sing things like the Byrd masses[1] in Latin. Douglas Guest arrived as organist in 1963 and he had an extensive knowledge of early Tudor music, dating from around the Reformation when they started using English texts. Guest increased the choir's repertory of this earlier music and his scholarship increased our understanding of how to sing it.

We started to sing more pieces in Latin and the Byrd masses previously sung at the abbey in English were, together with some Palestrina masses,[2] amongst the first things we sang in Latin at the Eucharist. That was the beginning of the reacceptance of Latin in the Anglican liturgy, so it was a fascinating time to be around.

Heather: That was quite a change. Did people object?

Leigh: There were probably some objections from the congregation, but most people didn't seem to mind at all. It's interesting that this was going on around the same time as the Second Vatican Council, when the Roman Catholic Mass began to be said in the vernacular instead of Latin, and we at the abbey were beginning to sing pieces in Latin instead of English, if that had been their original language.

Heather: You were firmly steeped in Anglicanism, both from your background and the experience of singing in the abbey.

Leigh: Yes. Before I went to the abbey I spent about two years in my local parish church choir, so I saw it from the parish point of view. Then again, I went back to a parish church after I left the abbey at fourteen. I was assistant organist at my local church because I'd started to learn the organ at school.

---

1 William Byrd (*c.* 1540-1623), was an English composer of the Renaissance.
2 Works by Giovanni Pierluigi da Palestrina (*c.* 1525-1594).

Heather: What were the differences between the abbey and the parish church you began to attend at fourteen?

Leigh: The cathedral and parish church traditions have a different emphasis. Your main job in the parish church, particularly at that time, was to lead the congregation. In "quires and places where they sing"[3] that is not the case. As a member of the congregation at cathedral Evensong, by all means join in the hymns and prayers, but otherwise the choir sings on your behalf. The French have the wonderful word *assister*; you *assiste* at the Mass, meaning you are there, part of it, but you're not necessarily taking part vocally; you're taking part mentally.

Heather: When you reached university age, what did you do?

Leigh: I was a choral scholar at King's College Cambridge between 1970 and 1973. David Willcocks was still there as Director of Music and my director of studies, and became the major influence in my musical life. After that I went to the Guildhall School of Music in London, commuting from Dorking in my first year and then, when my father went back to the abbey as librarian, I lived in Westminster. That allowed me time to get established on the London music scene.

I returned to the abbey choir in 1985 as a lay vicar – that's the same as a lay clerk or vicar choral – one of the adult professional members of the choir. Nowadays, the abbey and St Paul's Cathedral have twelve adult singers – four altos, four tenors and four basses. I was one of the four tenors at the abbey and I stayed there until I retired in 2013.

Heather: Did you have much interaction with the other choirs in London – St Paul's or the Roman Catholic Westminster Cathedral?

Leigh: I deputised for individual services at St Paul's when I came back to London, before I joined the abbey choir again. I also sang at Westminster Cathedral, only five hundred yards down the road, where I learnt to sing plainchant. You quickly got used to juggling books, because every piece of chant was in a different book, so you had a very large pile! Then the vast numbers of saints' days made it even more complicated to find your way around the music. More recently they've begun to reintroduce plainchant at the abbey as part of the liturgy; something entirely appropriate when you consider that, even now, Westminster Abbey has a longer history as a Roman Catholic church than as an Anglican church. And the place was built for singing chant – no question about it!

---

3 From the 1559 Prayer Book.

There's some cross-fertilisation of choir members between Westminster Abbey and Westminster Cathedral, not to mention the way that various organists have also moved between the two over the past twenty years.

Heather: So music transcends the differences?

Leigh: Oh, hugely. Although one is tied down by the times of the services, the men who are lay vicars at the abbey or lay clerks at the cathedral often find themselves going from one to the other, and occasionally even joining in their concerts.

Heather: What is your favourite service to sing?

Leigh: Probably Sunday Evensong when one can sing more elaborate settings and anthems. I also love psalmody, but it used rather to dominate weekday Evensong, particularly when I was a chorister and we still sang the complete psalms for the day. For instance, the psalm set for the fifteenth evening of the month is Psalm 78. That's seventy-three verses, plus the Gloria, and takes over fifteen minutes to sing. It's an absolutely fabulous psalm – "Hear my law, O ye people" – it gives a potted history of the peregrinations of the Jewish people.

Psalm singing to Anglican chant is one of the great joys of the Anglican Church, especially when using the Coverdale words found in the 1662 Book of Common Prayer. Coverdale may not be the most accurate translation but, like the King James Version of the Bible, the words are designed for an oral and aural tradition. Most of the congregation were not literate, so the language needed to be memorable. I've always thought that good liturgical language should be slightly "set apart" from the everyday and stick in the mind. Also, it should be designed to be read out in public. Whilst "Jesus said: 'Come and have breakfast'" is an entirely accurate modern translation from the Hebrew, the slightly softer "Come and eat" removes unwanted associations with kippers, toast and marmalade. Although the old Prayer Book language is slightly archaic – well, very archaic – it does actually stick, which is why I can quote the beginning of Psalm 78 off the top of my head.

Heather: What do you think is the purpose of music in a service?

Leigh: I have always thought that it is to provide a pause for contemplation – for creating a mood, if you like. An analogy I make is with English oratorio, like *Messiah*, made up from recitatives, arias and choruses. The recitative is designed to take the action forward. That's followed by an aria or chorus, which tends to pause on a particular emotion. So for instance, if you are working in the liturgy of the Church of England, it's right you should have anthems and so on, to concentrate your mind on the liturgical "theme". Obviously it is easier if you're dealing with some specific day like Good Friday, but also if you're in Advent or Lent, then the anthems are chosen to reflect the particular mood of those seasons. You're able to concentrate on the words, illustrated by the appropriate music, one hopes.

Heather: Do you have favourite pieces?

Leigh: Yes. For example, one anthem, which I think is the best I have ever sung, is a twentieth-century piece called *Viri Galilaei – Men of Galilee* – a setting by Patrick Gowers. It was written for Pentecost and consists of a powerful central section surrounded by ethereal alleluias. It is an extraordinary setting, aimed at very competent choirs, which is why you hear it sung very rarely.

Another that made a great impression on me is a Herbert Howells piece sung at John F. Kennedy's memorial service, *Take Him, Earth, for Cherishing*. The text is not actually biblical – it's a translation from Greek which predates the Christian era and again not an easy piece to sing.

Then, on the other hand, there are pieces that are simple and hit you between the eyes because they are so wonderful – the William Croft burial sentences: *I Am the Resurrection and the Life, Saith the Lord*, usually sung with *Thou Knowest, Lord, the Secrets of our Hearts* by Henry Purcell. Those are very, very moving.

Heather: Do you have favourite settings for Evensong?

Leigh: Oh yes. As a chorister I grew to know many of the twentieth-century English settings. Herbert Howells used to come to Evensong quite a lot when I was a chorister and would stand behind us and listen. "Howells in G" was a setting written when he was a young man studying with Edward Bairstow at York Minster in 1918. "Howells in B Minor" was written for the abbey in the 1950s, and there was also "Howells Westminster", written during the 1960s.

But I think my favourite Howells setting has to be his Gloucester service. It's in a mixture of F sharp major and F sharp minor and doesn't end with a huge, triumphal "Amen" – it just fades away into the ether. It's very beautiful and has to be one of the great Anglican settings. I also really like "Howells St Paul's", which I first sang as a choral scholar at King's Cambridge, and later we started doing it at the abbey too.

Heather: You must have sung at some memorable services?

Leigh: Yes, as a chorister I did one royal wedding which people hardly remember now – Angus Ogilvy and Princess Alexandra. Then in 1965 there was a huge televised service to celebrate the nine hundredth anniversary of the abbey's foundation by King Edward the Confessor. As a lay vicar I returned in time to do Prince Andrew and Sarah Ferguson's wedding in 1985 and later on, of course, in 2012 there was the Duke and Duchess of Cambridge.

Heather: Are they great occasions to sing at?

Leigh: Oh yes, they're great fun. I suppose the services which one remembers most, just because they were such huge occasions in the life of the British people, were two funerals, the Queen Mother and Princess Diana.

When I was a child, the British Empire was turning into the Commonwealth, and we sang celebration services for the independence of many Commonwealth countries. A lot of African countries which had been under British rule were now becoming their own places. We nearly always had to sing the new national anthem, in Swahili or whatever one of the thousands of tongues you find in the African content was appropriate. It was fascinating doing all those.

A service which has become much more important in recent years is the Anzac Day service which takes place on 25 April.[4] Australians and New Zealanders pour into the abbey. These are very moving services at which you may find, for example, the Turkish ambassador reading the words from the Anzac memorial in Gallipoli. There's a powerful feeling that the memory of the sacrifices that servicemen have made over the years needs to be kept alive.

Heather: Is there a lot of camaraderie in the choir?

Leigh: Oh yes, very much so. You can't have a group of twelve people like that who are required to work together without it. I suppose it's rather like

---

4 Marking the anniversary of the first major military action fought by Australian and New Zealand forces during the First World War.

a sports team. And it's also very important that you have respect for those people who are in charge of you. We had huge respect for James O'Donnell, Martin Baker and Simon Preston, for example.

Heather: You must have some amusing stories too?

Leigh: One or two! There was one marvellous Sunday Matins in the early 1990s when we were singing the Te Deum. It was a beautiful sunny morning and, suddenly, down the centre of the aisle marched the abbey's cat, Biggles. Because it was a lovely day, somebody had left the east cloister door open, so he just wandered in and came to see what was going on. He wandered down and was staring up at the choir. The canons' verger, Maureen Jupp, was a wonderful character and she was entirely equal to this. She came out of her stall just beside the canons, walked up to the cat, bowed to the altar, and with one arm scooped him up and processed round to the east cloister door and kicked him out. I'm quite sure the Americans sitting in the front row, slightly gaping, thought that this must be some obscure part of English religious ritual. But it was a marvellous sight!

Then there were the wonderful in-jokes, for example at Ronnie Barker's memorial service. Ronnie Corbett spoke and he had to stand on a special kneeler that was put in the pulpit so he could see over the top, and he drew attention to this. The very opening instruction in the service paper was that the Cross of Westminster was escorted by four candles, a sideways allusion to one of the well-known sketches from their TV show, *The Two Ronnies*.[5]

Heather: How would you sum up your attitude to Anglican music?

Leigh: Since I knew we were going to be talking about it, I've been asking myself "What are the main joys I got out of it?" I think one of the real joys I've had is the extraordinary variety of music-making that I have encountered. My personal churchmanship perhaps verges towards the higher end, but I think it's very important that the Church of England should continue to espouse both ends of the scale. But I'm saddened when I see the words of whatever translation of the Bible you happen to be reading treated as a rulebook and as the only possible way of looking at things. Saying, "Let's praise the Lord" can turn into as much of a formula as saying, "Lord, in your mercy, hear our prayer." We've always used formulae in Anglican services and it's also important that people actually think about why they are doing what they're doing in services.

---

5 This refers to a sketch where the shopkeeper misunderstands what the customer wants – is it "four candles", or "fork handles"?

I've been very lucky to be around during what has been a time of great change in liturgical terms. I have loved singing Book of Common Prayer Matins and Evensong, but Eucharistic worship has become much more important to me, and it's central to what I value of church worship. It's also nice to find that the way in which the Eucharist and the Roman Catholic Mass are offered is very similar now, and I feel entirely at home in either tradition.

Heather: Whither church music, do you think?

Leigh: Within the Anglican Communion I am a little nervous for church music within the parish set-up. However, I think we are incredibly lucky in England that we have cathedrals, many of which have professional or semi-professional choirs, and a lot of them have very sensibly started employing girls as well as boys. Musically speaking, I think singing as a chorister is a wonderful training, even if you don't use it in later life. If you drop it at thirteen it's still a wonderful thing to have done, and it's amazing how many who have dropped music come back to it when they're older.

Heather: It gets in your soul?

Leigh: Yes. You can't really use anything else but the words of the Magnificat: "My soul doth magnify the Lord." And that word "magnify" is something you can say about music's function within the liturgy, because that's exactly what it does.